# California Ghosting

## True Accounts of Hauntings in the Golden State

### Preston E. Dennett

*Illustrated by Christine Kesara Dennett*

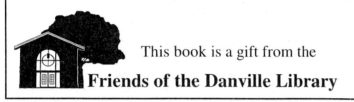

Schiller Publishing Ltd.

4880 Lower Valley Road, Atglen, PA 19310 USA

*proofreader needed!*

# Dedication

To my mother, Nancy, whose death launched
my own journey into the world of the paranormal.

Library of Congress Cataloging-in-Publication Data

Dennett, Preston E., 1965-
 California ghosts: true accounts of hauntings in
the Golden State / by Preston E. Dennett.
    p. cm.
  ISBN 0-7643-1972-8 (pbk.)
1. Ghosts--California. I. Title.
BF1472.U6 D46 2004
133.1'09794--dc22

                                    2003019880

Designed by Mark David Bowyer
Type set in Marigold/Korinna BT

ISBN: 0-7643-1972-8
Printed in China

Published by Schiffer Publishing Ltd.
4880 Lower Valley Road
Atglen, PA 19310
Phone: (610) 593-1777; Fax: (610) 593-2002
E-mail: Info@schifferbooks.com
Please visit our web site catalog at
**www.schifferbooks.com**
We are always looking for people to write books
on new and related subjects. If you have an
idea for a book, please contact us at the above
address. Need a copy editor.

This book may be purchased from the
publisher.
Include $3.95 for shipping.
Please try your bookstore first.
You may write for a free catalog.

In Europe, Schiffer books are distributed by
Bushwood Books
6 Marksbury Avenue
Kew Gardens
Surrey TW9 4JF England
Phone: 44 (0) 20 8392 8585
Fax: 44 (0) 20 8392 9876
E-mail: Bushwd@aol.com
Free postage in the UK. Europe: air mail at
cost.

# Contents

# Acknowledgments

There is a long list of people who deserve special thanks for their support. I would like to thank the scores of witnesses whose accounts are included in this book; without their courage to step forth and tell their stories, this book would never have become a reality. I would also like to thank my family and friends for putting up with my obsession. Finally, I would like to thank the artist, Christine Kesara Dennett for proof-reading the manuscript, conduct- *Doh!* ing a few of the interviews, and mostly for her incredible ability to illustrate the unseen.

# Note to the Reader

The stories you are about to read are true. The events really happened. As you read, you will follow firsthand an investigation that will lead directly into the heart of the Unknown. There you will find a strange world of seemingly impossible events. You will read fascinating accounts of haunted houses and ghostly apparitions of all types. You will hear stories that will boggle the mind. Some of the stories are sad, some are happy. Some are funny, some are scary. Some are downright bone-chilling. But most importantly, they are all true, and are told in the witnesses' own words.

You will experience the thoughts, feelings, and emotions of those people, who, for no reason they can fathom, have been plunged into the realm of the unexplained. You will be a silent witness to their journey through the world of the paranormal. So keep your mind open. Don't be too skeptical. The accounts you read just might change your views about those strange things we call ghosts.

# Introduction

Of course, ghosts are real. I have talked to hundreds of people who don't have the luxury of disbelief. They have seen ghosts themselves and it is their accounts that make up the body of this book. The stories they told me have shattered my skepticism about ghosts. They spoke of furniture moving mysteriously, doors opening and closing, ghostly footsteps, disappearing objects, glowing apparitions, ghosts that answer phones, footsteps, ghosts that give loving hugs, ghosts that attack the terrified witnesses, child ghosts, poltergeists, and much more. I heard stories that challenged everything I knew. After studying the accounts it became clear that ghosts are not only real, but they provide incontrovertible evidence that *some aspect* of the human organism survives death.

The people in this book have interacted with ghosts to an astonishing degree. They have not only seen ghosts, they have heard them, felt them, and even smelled them. They have exchanged words and relayed messages. They have been hugged, poked, slapped, pushed, choked, and even possessed.

After interviewing the many witnesses and visiting the places where ghosts haunt, I have come to know ghosts quite well. I have seen how hauntings begin, how they progress and how they end. I have watched firsthand as people living with ghosts struggle to understand what is happening to them.

I used to be extremely dubious of ghosts. In fact, I was so unconvinced that even after I saw a ghost, I still didn't believe in them. It was 1984, two weeks after my mother died. My family and friends were gathering for her service. As I stood waiting in the driveway, a full color apparition of my mother appeared. I saw her from four feet away for about ten seconds before she faded away. I literally could not believe my eyes and assumed I was hallucinating. I told no one. After all, ghosts weren't real.

Then, a few years later in 1988, a close friend confided to me that her house was haunted. I told her she must be either joking or crazy. However, she insisted that she was serious and proceeded to tell me a story that pierced through the thick armor of disbelief. Then I remembered my own secret ghost sighting. Could ghosts actually be real?

I was now on a quest to learn the truth about ghosts. My friend's story was only the first of an amazing series of stories told to me by a vast number of Californians. It didn't take me long to realize that my skepticism had blinded me to the reality of ghosts. I was *not* happy to find out that ghosts were real. It meant a huge change in the way I thought about the world.

And so this book was born.

All of the cases in this book take place throughout California, in peoples' homes, in apartment buildings, business offices, graveyards, and outside on the street – in other words, everywhere. Several of the cases are still ongoing.

While the book presents a wide variety of ghostly visitations, the last five chapters involve cases of extreme hauntings in which people's encounters with ghosts reached the final stage of attempted possession.

Some of the witnesses whose stories are told in the book have allowed their real names to be used. Others have insisted upon complete anonymity and have been given pseudonyms. Needless to say, all of them now believe in ghosts. They will be the first to tell you that ghosts are real. The evidence for this is in the exciting pages that follow.

# 1 – Ghosts of the Indian Burial Ground

Topanga Canyon is a small community nestled among the Santa Monica Mountains in southern California. Surrounded on three sides by the sprawling city of Los Angeles, Topanga remains an outpost of country, largely because the wilderness is protected by Topanga State Park.

Topanga Canyon is well-known to have been the native habitat of the Chumash Indians. The Chumash name for Topanga was, "Where the mountains meet the sea."

The center of Topanga is perhaps the best known of all the local Chumash Indian settlements. About five or ten stores and shops have been built over what used to be a huge Chumash settlement.

The caves above Santa Maria creek are also known to have been used by the Chumash Indians. Located amid the poison oak, overgrown chaparral, and steep cliffs are six or seven caves. Evidence of the settlement is still apparent in the form of smooth, rounded grind holes used for grinding buckwheat into flour. Further evidence belying the settlement are scorch marks on the tops of the caves.

Another larger Chumash Indian settlement was located in-between the Santa Maria settlement and the Topanga Center settlement. About halfway up the street Entrada, lies a street called Colina, which is separated into upper and lower sections, both of which are located on former Chumash settlements.

The fact that Native Americans really lived in Topanga really became evident to me as a young child, when I was at a friend's house on lower Colina. We were playing with matchbox cars in the backyard, creating little driveways and roads. As we were digging, my friend uncovered a shiny white object. He brushed off the dirt and we looked at it, amazed. It was a perfectly formed arrowhead. It was about four inches long and made of white flint.

I learned later that a local resident collected a number of Chumash Indian artifacts in his home. My friend donated his arrowhead to the man's collection.

With all these settlements, it is only logical that one would expect to have some sort of burial ground. And of course, there was one, and it was quite large. But one would not expect homes to be built right on it.

But in fact, that is exactly what happened. When the burial ground was discovered, the property was already sold and developed with private homes. Only a portion of the burial ground was preserved as a part of Topanga State Park.

The unfortunate residents whose homes were built on the land had no idea that they lived on or next to a Chumash Indian burial ground. At first it didn't seem to matter. That is, not until several of them began to experience dramatic paranormal activity. At least four of the households in the area of the burial ground have experienced phenomena such as objects moving by themselves, unexplained knockings, ghostly footsteps, windows breaking without cause, and more.

The main witnesses to this case have elected to remain anonymous, simply because they don't want people to think that they're crazy. I shall call them the Henderson family.

It was in the early 1970s when the family of five moved into their brand new home on Colina. They lived there for three years with no ghostly activity at all, until one day in 1973, when a very dramatic incident occurred. It was daytime, and Mrs. Henderson and her four-year-old daughter were standing at one end of the living room. Nobody else was in the room.

They watched in stunned silence as a pillow on the couch rose up by itself, and flew across the room towards them. As Mrs. Henderson says, "The one thing that was really strange was when my daughter and I were in the living room and we were maybe eight feet away from the couch. And a pillow flew off our couch and onto the floor. And you know, it's the strangest thing I've ever seen. There's no accounting for it at all...it was on the couch, leaning against the back of the couch, and it flew across the room. And it landed on the floor. It came right near where we were. It was like somebody had thrown it. It was just like that.

"It was unbelievable. It was like, 'Did that really happen?' But my daughter saw it happen too. I mean, I couldn't have imagined it because we both saw it happen. And she still remembers it. She still remembers the color of the pillow. It was really weird. I keep thinking about that. Did that really happen? Yes, it did. I'm sure it happened."

That incident marked the beginning of a series of unexplained events that left the entire family baffled as to what was going on in their home. Shortly following the pillow incident, they began to hear strange noises in the basement. Sometimes it sounded like furniture being moved upstairs when nobody was there. Other times, it was a strange tapping noise on the basement wall. It happened over and over again, usually at the same time every night.

Before long, the Henderson family became used to the bizarre ritual of searching their house for the source of the mysterious knocking sounds. As Mrs. Henderson says, "We used to hear tapping noises down on the basement wall at night. And if you were down in the basement, it sounded like our chairs were being moved. It sounded like that. But the tapping on the wall – that was weird. It happened about the same time every night. We slept in the basement, and we were convinced that something was going on in that house.

"The tapping, it could have been...it could have been...I don't know, the pipes? No, it wasn't the pipes. We would have heard it if it was the pipes. I don't know what the tapping came from."

Every night it was the same thing. Around eight o'clock the noises would come. Almost always it was the tapping sound, and usually there were three taps in a row. The entire family was mystified by the noises. Although Mr. Henderson was skeptical that their house was haunted, he still had no explanation for the levitation of the pillow, or the knocking noises.

In search of answers, Mrs. Henderson decided to brave ridicule and disbelief and ask her neighbors if they had experienced anything strange or unusual. To her surprise, she discovered that at least two of her neighbors were experiencing similar paranormal activity.

The neighbors immediately next door said that they were occasionally interrupted by the sound of footsteps traveling through their home. They would rush to see who was there, but the room would always be empty. A few times, however, the footsteps came when people were present in the room. The residents were able to pinpoint the source of the sound and could actually follow the sound of the footsteps as they moved through the house. They never saw who made the footsteps. The intruder was completely invisible.

The next house down the road also experienced an event that the residents feel was unexplained. One day, an upstairs window was shattered under very mysterious circumstances. Although they tried to blame the accident on the weather or pranksters, they were unable to do so. They couldn't figure out what had shattered their window.

Alone, any one of these events might seem inconsequential. But taken together, they form an alarming pattern.

The Henderson family had moved into a newly built house. Nobody had ever lived there before them. Nobody had died in the house, nor had any great tragedy occurred. Mrs. Henderson couldn't find any reason why their particular house was haunted. And when she found out that the neighbors were also having unexplained experiences, she figured that there must be something about the general area that was causing the haunting. The only thing she could think of was the Chumash Indian burial ground which was a mere stone's throw away from her house.

A few years later, the Hendersons sold their house and moved away. The new residents remodeled the house and added on a room. As far as the Hendersons know, the new residents have not experienced anything strange, nor have the neighbors reported any further activity.

That is not to say that the Indian ghosts are gone. There are still indications that Chumash Indians are not too happy to find their sacred burial ground desecrated by the new houses that have been built all around the area.

After asking several other people in the area if they have experienced any ghost activity, I discovered yet another family whose house was haunted. Their home, it turned out, was built virtually on the burial ground. This home is a few houses down the road of the first house, however it is still within the range of the burial ground. In fact, their backyard is on the burial ground itself. Even today, the burial mounds are clearly visible.

Pamela Mitchell (not her real name) was only nine years old when she and her parents lived in the house along Entrada. And although they lived there only a short time, it was long enough for Pamela to grow to hate the house.

When they purchased the property, the home was little more than a shack with a garage. But they knocked it all down and built a large two-story house.

To pass the time, Pamela used to go into her backyard and play. Unfortunately, the only place she could play was directly over the Chumash Indian burial ground. She was at first enchanted by the multitudes of stones set up in little piles and formations. But for some reason she didn't quite understand, it also scared her. Several times she would be overcome with the feeling that something or someone was watching her. Although she never actually saw anything, an ominous presence would permeate the area and Pamela would run as fast as she could to the safety of her home.

As Pamela says, "On Entrada, just beyond second Encina was our house. On the land there was a little area of rocks, pointed ones of different shapes. Well, I used to go and play in the rocks right where there was that little rounded area of rocks where the burial ground was.

"Boy, did I used to run. It was more like a feeling. I would always feel like they were there, and I would run. I was eight, nine. And I would just jam."

Pamela's experiences in the burial ground occurred several times until she became frightened of the area and avoided it. However, that didn't stop the problem. Pamela had begun to sense something strange about the house itself.

The house was practically brand new and there was certainly nothing outwardly wrong with it. Pamela couldn't figure out why, but the house actually terrified her. It began with just a creepy feeling. She didn't like to be left alone in the house.

Pamela's parents hadn't had any experiences, and they attributed her fears to an overactive imagination. Pamela, however, knew that there was a reason she was so afraid. She had good reason to believe that their house was haunted. When she was alone in her bedroom at night, Pamela began to have some very spooky experiences.

As she says, "My bedroom was way on the other side of the house, and I was so frightened in that house that I would sleep in the living room almost nightly. I used to think I saw things. I would wake up and scream and nothing would come out of my mouth. I'd be so freaked out about it."

Pam grew to hate and fear and the house and she was tremendously relieved when her parents decided to move. As far as she remembers, the fact that she was having problems with ghosts was not the reason for the move. Evidently, her parents simply wanted to move.

None of them had any idea that the other houses nearby were also experiencing ghost activity.

This case is unique in that the haunting was so severe as to extend into several homes. However, there is evidence that the Indians are haunting the hills of Topanga. One psychic who visited Topanga told me that he sensed the presence of Indians roaming the mountains. Another lady I know was hiking through the area of the burial ground when she sensed a group of very angry Native American spirits who wanted her out of the area. Needless to say, she left. Yet another witness reports that she was meditating in the area when she sensed the presence of a small Indian girl, looking at her sadly. And still another witness told me that he was jogging in the State Park when he sensed the presence of Indians who seemed angry that he was intruding on their area.

I later learned from a secondhand source that another location in Topanga also suffered a severe poltergeist infestation. Upon investigation, they learned that their home was also built upon a Chumash burial ground. Their home was investigated by a UCLA parapsychology department and was the inspiration for the blockbuster movie *Poltergeist*.

So as one can see, the area is still somewhat active. This case proves that if there is one way to upset the spirits, it is to build homes over a sacred burial ground.

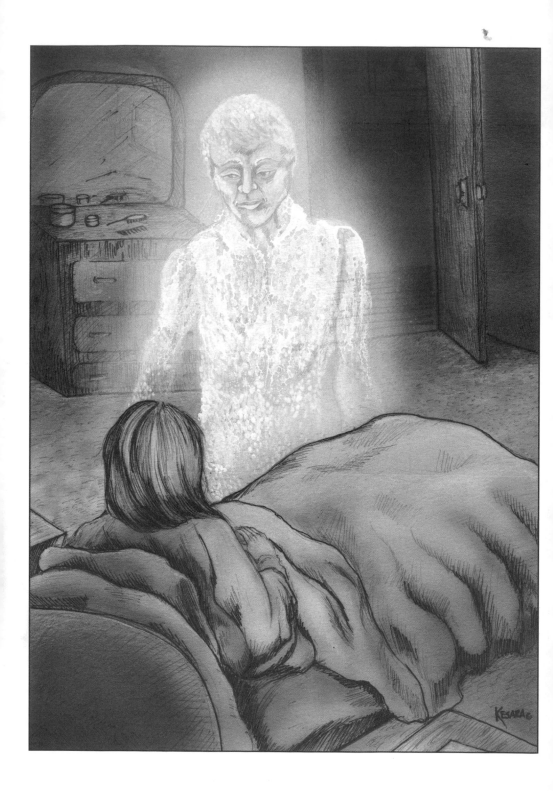

# 2 – Woken Up By a Ghost

Longtime Topanga resident, Laura L. lives in a little house which is nestled above Topanga creek in the middle of the canyon. She has lived there peacefully for many years. She makes a modest living giving music lessons and working at a nearby health food store.

Laura didn't believe or disbelieve in ghosts. She never really gave them much thought, that is, until one time in the late 1970s, when one woke her up in the middle of the night.

At one time or another, we have all had the experience of being woken up from a sound sleep by someone shaking us. Almost invariably, however, when we wake up we recognize the person who woke us up, and he or she doesn't usually glow in the dark and disappear before our very eyes.

This is precisely what happened to Laura. There was nobody in the house and Laura was sleeping peacefully when she woke up because she felt that someone was standing next to her bed, leaning over her. Naturally, she was a bit frightened and thought at first that she might be dreaming. So she shook herself completely awake, fully expecting the figure to disappear. But to her surprise, it was still there. And not only that, the figure glowed with an eerie white light and he was staring at Laura with a radiant smile.

Laura explains, "I was asleep, and in my sleep I saw this man leaning over me in bed. And I got scared, but he looked really beautiful. He had this really joyous kind of look on his face – a really nice kind of look. And he was really bright. But I got scared, and I kind of shook myself awake. I forced myself to wake up and open my eyes, and I still saw him. Then he kind of vanished into thin air. He started moving kind of like stop-action. And then he was gone.

"He had silver-gray hair, and was kind of good-looking. I guess fiftiesh."

Laura tried to pass off the experience as a particularly vivid dream, except that it was totally unlike any dream she has had, before or after this incident. First of all, Laura woke up and the man was still there. And the man was very strange because he glowed so brightly and had a strange expression of contentment on his face. And the way the man disappeared was also strange. Laura used the famous painting, *Nude Descending a Staircase*, by the French Cubist, Marcel Duchamp, to illustrate the way the man disappeared. The painting is an abstract, cubist portrait of a person. Laura described the man that she saw as being normal-looking, except for the fact that he faded away slowly. Like the person in the painting, it was as if the man was composed of sections. The man disappeared section by section in a sort of stop-action motion, as if he were composed of pixels on a television screen.

Laura was very impressed by how beautiful the man was, and his odd expression of joy. The man looked so friendly that she was surprised by her own reaction of fear. But as she says, she didn't know who he was or why he had woken her up out of a sound sleep.

At first, Laura didn't think she had seen a ghost. The incident was just too strange to fit into her belief system, so she filed it away in the back of her mind for later reference. It wasn't until about ten years later, when the subject of ghosts came up, that Laura remembered her experience.

As far as Laura knows, nobody has ever died in her home. But she does admit that the house is quite old, built in the 1930s, and that many people have lived there in the past. To her knowledge, however, she's the only one to be woken up in the middle of the night by a glowing, smiling man who disappeared right before her eyes.

# 3 – The Ghost Who Answered the Phone

"I don't want people to think I'm crazy."

The above sentence, a quote from the central witness to this case, is the main reason why most people won't tell anyone about the ghost experiences they have had. Millions of intelligent, competent people see ghosts and spirits, but they won't talk about them, and if they do, they often desire to remain anonymous. Often it seems that people are more afraid of what other people will think of their ghostly encounter than of the encounter itself.

This is sometimes understandable because there are occasions when something so bizarre happens, the witnesses can hardly believe it themselves. How can they expect anyone else to believe?

Such is the case in the following account. A mother and her two daughters lived alone in a house high in the mountains of Topanga, California. The eldest daughter, Sarah Webster (not her real name) was the unfortunate witness to most of the ghost activity. Sarah insisted upon anonymity because she doesn't want to deal with people who don't believe her, including the people in her own family.

She tried to convince her family that there was a ghost in their house, but her sister and mother looked upon the subject with contempt. To them, the idea that their house could be haunted was preposterous.

The ordeal began one day in the mid 1970s when Sarah was alone in the house, and she thought she heard someone coughing in the back room. The first few times, she simply ignored the sound. But occasionally, she would hear the coughing very clearly, and she knew she was completely alone. Each time, she would dash to locate to the sound, but there was never anybody there. It happened several times and she began to suspect that there was a ghost in the house.

She tried to tell her family, "We have a ghost." To her surprise, nobody believed her.

But Sarah had no doubt about the ghost after a particularly unnerving experience. Again, she was alone in the house when she heard the sound of a man coughing. She cocked her head and listened intently. What she heard chilled her to the bone. As she says, "I heard this coughing. And then I heard somebody go into the bathroom and close the door, spit into the toilet, and flush it. And I freaked out. I was like, 'Aaaahhh!!!' and I ran out. I don't even remember what I did, but I know that I left. And I didn't go home until there was somebody else there."

Sarah thought about telling her family what happened, but knowing that they wouldn't believe her, she just kept it to herself. Hearing the sound of the ghost coughing, however, was still extremely frightening. She remembers leaving the house more than once after hearing the ghost, but after a couple of years, she realized that the sounds had stopped. She figured that the ghost was gone and thought no more about it.

Years later, everyone had moved out and the house was being rented to a young couple. The new tenants had never heard any of the stories and had no reason to suspect that the house was haunted. Then in April of 1989, the ghost returned.

The wife was alone in the house. She turned on the radio loudly and went into the bathroom to take a shower. She was in the middle of the shower when the phone rang. She decided to just ignore the phone and continue her shower. Whoever it was would call back. The phone rang three or four times and then stopped. She assumed that the caller had simply hung up.

Her husband, however, was the caller. He had dialed his home number, heard the phone ring, and then heard somebody pick up the phone. As he waited for his wife to say hello, he heard a certain song playing on the radio in the background. Then to his surprise, whoever answered the phone hung up on him.

Meanwhile, his wife had quickly finished her shower and was drying off when the phone rang again. Her husband was on the line and he asked angrily, "Who's there?! Who's there?!"

"It's just me," she said.

"Well, somebody just picked up the phone," he said.

"No," she said. "You must have dialed the wrong number."

"No," her husband replied. "I hear the same song playing on the radio."

His wife told him that she had heard the phone ring, but she assumed that whoever it was had hung up. But he said that it was he who had just called, and somebody else answered the phone and hung up on him.

They were both perplexed by the incident, but both of them jumped to the obvious conclusion; there must have been an intruder in the house. She checked the entire house, but as she suspected, she was alone. All the doors were locked. They had never had any problems with intruders before. It just didn't make any sense. Nevertheless, she became paranoid about someone being in the house while she was taking a shower.

She mentioned the incident to Sarah and asked if they had ever had any intruders before. Sarah listened carefully and before she knew what she was doing, she said, "Oh, it's probably just the ghost."

Sarah was concerned that the couple might be somewhat frightened by this revelation. Instead, they were actually relieved to find that the intruder was merely a ghost and not a physical intruder. I asked Sarah if anybody had ever died in the house and she told me that, in fact, two people had died in the house. One of them, however, suffered from chronic emphysema. While he was visiting, his condition forced him to make frequent trips to the bathroom where he would cough and spit into the toilet. Afterwards, he would, of course, flush the toilet. He died in the house in the early 1970s, and Sarah remarks that the coughing she heard and the coughing of the man who died in the house sounded exactly the same. And when she had the experience of hearing the bathroom door close, a man spit and a toilet flush, she was certain it was his spirit.

When she heard the tenants' story, she was surprised that the ghost was still around. But she was also happy that at last she had confirmation. Finally, there were some other witnesses. She wasn't the only one who had met the ghost.

In this case, the ghost was able to close doors, flush toilets, answer phones as well as produce sounds of coughing and spitting. This case is typical of many hauntings. In some cases of sudden death, it seems that the deceased do not know that they are dead. They continue on with the same behavior that they exhibited before their death. Because of the shock of death, they sometimes have trouble thinking clearly enough to realize that they are in the next dimension.

This seems to be the situation in this case. Today, the haunting has apparently ended, and the house has been sold. The new residents have no idea that the house was once haunted by a restless spirit.

# 4 – The Ghost Who Came to Bed

What would you do if you woke up one night feeling somebody crawling into bed with you, and when you looked, nobody was there? And what if it happened not once or twice, but over and over again? What would you do?

Sally Sanders (not her real name) did not have the luxury of forethought when the experience happened to her. But she did have the advantage of having been raised in a haunted house.

Sally grew up in a small town in Nebraska. She lived with her family in her grandmother's home, which had been converted from an old hotel. The hotel was the first structure built in the town, and it was built right along the railroad after the tracks were laid down. As Sally grew up, family members would regularly report having seen apparitions of dead relatives. Once Sally heard someone come into the house, but nobody was there when she looked. According to Sally, everyone in the town knew the place was haunted, and nearly everyone had a story to tell of the ghosts they had seen there.

Sally never once saw a ghost, but because of her relatives, she had no reason to doubt their existence. She was therefore more prepared than most people to deal with a ghostly encounter.

Years later, Sally moved away from the haunted hotel and made her residence in Merced, California. She had been living there with her husband for only a few months when she began having strange experiences.

Every once in a while, Sally would wake up in bed to find someone crawling into bed with her when nobody was there. It felt to her just like there was a person laying next to her on the bed. The bed would creak and the blankets would rustle. It was all just too strange for Sally to handle.

As she says, "It was really funny, but it scared me. I never laughed. When I was alone and I would get into bed and I would feel something get on the bed, turn, and lay down on his side of the bed. And all I would do was get up and go into the other room. And I would spend the night in there. It was kind of scary, but it didn't scare me too badly, maybe because I really didn't have any place to go. I don't know what it was exactly. It was kind of weird."

The first time it happened, Sally was scared and upset. But she figured it was a unique experience, and that it wouldn't happen again. She was wrong. It happened again, and then again. Each time it was the same thing. She would feel someone slip into bed and when she looked, nobody was there. Each time, she got more and more frightened, and when it happened, Sally always slept in the other room. Although the experience scared her badly, it was just infrequent enough that she was able to put up with it. But the experience occurred again, and Sally became concerned that their ghost, if that's what it was, would never go away.

So Sally decided to try an experiment. Since the ghost always lay down in the same spot, she decided to move the bed to the other side of the room. She was hoping it would make the ghost go away. Instead, it seemed to make things worse.

As she says, "It stayed so long that I felt as though it was a bad experience. So I turned my bed around. It was that same spot. It was where the end of the bed hit that spot that the ghost used to lay. One night it touched my toe. I felt it. I actually felt it! It felt like something. It was weird. It felt like something brushed my toe."

At this point, the haunting seemed to increase. Moving the bed around had evidently only made the ghost angry. Sally, however, decided to stick it out, but only for one reason; they had plans to move out of the house very soon. Sally was glad to be leaving. The ghost was driving her crazy. She knew she couldn't live with it much longer. That's when the ghost attacked. As she says, "It was about two weeks before we were to move, and I woke up one night, or my husband woke me up, and I couldn't breathe. I had this feeling that something was on my chest. I felt like something was sitting on my chest. My husband woke me up, and he said that I was making all this noise. It was as if I couldn't breathe, and it was really aggravating me. And he woke me up. But it felt like something was crushing me, almost crushing me like I was an accordion.

"It was really weird. My husband at one time when he was younger, he was in some sort of witchcraft thing. And he put some sort of thing – some sort of protection around me. It never bothered me again, but we stayed there only another two weeks."

Sally found the experience utterly terrifying, and she was very happy to be moving. She never experienced anything like that after she left. She doesn't know who the ghost was, or why he kept coming to her bed. She didn't really care. She was content to forget about the experience as best as she could. If she had it her way, she would never remember it again.

# 5 – Embraced By a Ghost

For many people, encountering a ghost can be terrifying. The unfortunate witnesses would prefer not to have encountered the ghost at all. There are many reasons for this. One might be that people are afraid of what they don't understand. And when they are plunged involuntarily into the world of the unexplained, along with the confusion comes a very real fear. The subject of ghosts conjures up images of evil spirits and demons bent on possessing one's body and stealing one's soul.

When people, see, hear, feel or somehow sense a ghost, they don't think that the ghost might be more like Casper, The Friendly Ghost.

Casper was a character in a children's cartoon. He was the ghost of a child, and unlike his older ghostly peers who were obsessed with scaring people, Casper only wanted to make friends. During every episode, Casper was able to make friends only with those who didn't know that he was a ghost. He was invariably disappointed because most of the people he met were terrified of him, just because he was a ghost. He couldn't understand why he was so scary. He was just a child who wanted to make friends. So what if he was a ghost?

As unrealistic as all this sounds, just such an event may be much more common than is generally thought. Child ghosts are not uncommon. Often the child ghosts are sad, forlorn little souls, lost and forgotten. Nothing is more tragic than a child ghost.

The ghost of one small child may very well have haunted the house of a family in Canyon Country, California. The instant they moved into their home, strange events began to occur. The adventure started in 1977 and continued until 1981. The turn of events so impressed Jan Luber, the central witness to this case, that she wrote down all of her experiences, so that she would never forget them.

She always hoped that someday she would find someone who was interested in her story. She had made the mistake of telling the wrong people before, those who disbelieved her despite her insistence that she was telling the truth. They tried to tell her she had imagined the whole thing, but Jan just told them, "Listen, you haven't had my experiences," and leaves it at that. She doesn't try to convince anybody, and is not out for publicity. Jan was enthusiastic to share her story with people who would believe her. And so she allowed her story to be included in this collection. This is her story in her own words, which she calls: 'The Invisible Observer.'

Jan: It was a few years after the haunting that in the course of conversation with my youngest daughter, Lisa, I discovered that I wasn't the only one who had experienced the "presence" that had lived with us. Although my husband and my older daughter had never been touched by the spirit, Lisa and I gratefully shared our experiences with each other, because while the events were taking place, I chose not to say anything, as I didn't want to alarm the family, and Lisa never mentioned it because she didn't want to be ridiculed.

It all began that afternoon seven years ago when I first saw the house. It had been a grueling day of looking through several houses and feeling increasingly disappointed. The real estate lady and I were on our own that afternoon as my husband was working, and the children were in school. When we arrived at the house, the real estate lady explained to me that the house had been on the market for quite a while and mentioned the fact that it was several thousand dollars more than we had indicated we wanted to spend. My opinion was, it never hurts to look.

When we walked in the front door I stood in the entry way and a feeling washed over me and I knew I would live in that house. It was as though it had been looking for me. All the drapes were tightly closed and I simply peered into the rooms with the compelling knowledge that this was where I would live.

Later that evening I excitedly described the house to my husband, and we poured over our budget to see if it was possible for us to make an offer. After seeing the house, he agreed that it was everything I had described, and we decided to go and buy it.

Moving day finally arrived and after the former owners had vacated, I wandered through the house and felt a discernible sadness that emanated from the rooms. I flung open the drapes only to realize that it seemed they had not been drawn open for years. How strange, not to let the California sunshine pour into the rooms. All of us were extremely busy cleaning, unpacking and putting things away. I mentioned to the family that I thought the house was "sad" only to have them stare at me as if I had lost my mind!

The first few weeks were uneventful as we settled into our new home. We were occupied with scrubbing and painting, and the only disturbing event was the fact that Lisa said she didn't like her new room, even though she never stated logical reasons. Later I would know why. Also Lisa, then almost twelve, flatly refused to stay at home alone, even if it involved only a few minutes while I ran out to the store.

After pushing furniture around in an attempt to find the most comfortable arrangement, we agreed to put my dearly loved piano in the entry way near the living room which was actually the end of the hall which went back to the bedroom. The piano was to be a part of my first experience with the spirit.

One evening I found myself alone in the house which was a bit unusual. Since it had been three weeks since I touched the piano, here was my perfect opportunity. No one at home, and I could play to my heart's delight. As it was arranged, when sitting at the piano, my back was to the hall. I had played a couple of pieces when I began to feel there was someone standing at the end of the hall. I glanced over my shoulder every once in a while, fully expecting to see someone, only to tell myself I was acting foolish. Suddenly the family burst through the door and I quickly forgot about my experience.

As I found out later, Lisa had been experiencing the same feelings of someone or something watching her.

As the months went by I adjusted to having the "invisible observer" around and had decided that this spirit really enjoyed my piano playing as weeks could go by without my feeling of a presence, and as soon as I was alone playing the piano, I could feel the spirit at the end of the hall. On occasion, it would come up the hall and stand directly behind me which would quickly end my concert.

During these visitations I never felt any particular fear, even though at times I became uneasy because of the fact that it was, after all, something I couldn't see but could definitely feel.

At one point Lisa agreed to spend the evening alone while my husband and I went out if her friend Carrie could spend the night. During the evening Lisa decided to go up the block to borrow something from one of her other friends and Carrie said she would stay in the house and play the piano. As Lisa came back home she realized that Carrie was sitting on the curb out in front of the house. Carrie told Lisa she had been playing the piano when suddenly there was something there with her, and went on to explain she would never stay alone in the house again.

One evening I was using the typewriter in one of the bedrooms we had converted to an office. My back was to the closed door and I was deep in thought. Suddenly I felt someone standing behind me, and felt annoyed at being disturbed by my husband. I finally turned around ready to make my desire to be alone known, only to find no one there. Having for the moment put the spirit out of my mind, I figured my husband was playing a joke on me. A few minutes later I once again felt the presence of someone, only to turn around and find no one. By now my train of thought was gone and I was struggling to get back into my work, when the presence was back and much stronger. All of a sudden I felt as though arms were attempting to encircle me from behind. That did it! I was up and out of the room but still chose not to mention it to the family.

Later as I was reflecting on the experience, I came to an enlightening conclusion. Our spirit was a child because of the height of where the arms had tried to encircle me. I also realized it hadn't been trying to hurt me, but simply wanted to hug me. Also, for some reason, I knew it was a girl. A sad wandering child spirit in need of love.

After that time I found myself seeking out the spirit as I played the piano, and at times, I would speak to it. The uneasiness I felt had been replaced by curiosity. Why would a child spirit be in our house? What sadness had she experienced? And how could I help her?

As time went by I became accustomed to having our "invisible observer" by my side or standing right behind me as I played the piano, but still I never mentioned it to my family or friends. It was my secret.

My older daughter got married and left home, and shortly thereafter, Lisa had the opportunity to go and live in Anchorage with my sister. Suddenly the house was empty and the children were gone. The "spirit child" seemed to appear less often as though there was some connection she had with our children.

One night I woke up about 2:30 a.m. to an eerie moaning sound that seemed to emanate from all over the house. At first it was a very low sound and I wasn't alarmed. It would seem to go away for a while and then return a little bit louder. I finally woke up my husband and asked him what he thought the sound was. We got out of bed and began to prowl through the house looking for the source. There seemed to be no source; it was simply everywhere and in every room. Thinking it might be air in the water pipes, we checked out the plumbing only to find it functioning properly. By this time the sound was very loud, and I was getting quite upset. Then suddenly it was gone.

It was a few days later when I realized that our spirit was gone and I can only surmise that the sounds we had heard a few nights earlier had something to do with its leave-taking. I trust it went on to better things, and perhaps in some small way we had helped it.

I find myself now sometimes thinking of the spirit and realizing that when I'm in the house alone, I am really alone. I must admit there are times when I truly miss giving piano recitals for the "invisible observer."

And so ends Jan Luber's account of the haunting of her home. Not only did at least three people feel a presence, but Jan actually felt the ghost embrace her from behind. She said that the spirit would stand behind her for as long as a half hour while she played the piano. She also mentioned that she never felt the spirit in the front section of the house. It always stayed in the back part of the house. I asked her to describe again what it felt like to be hugged by a ghost. Says Jan, "It was like a presence. And finally, after about the third time, I could feel it. I mean, if I had turned around and seen a person putting their arms around me, such as one of my children, it would not have surprised me in the least. It was that strong. And I wished with all my heart that I hadn't just jumped up. It freaked me out obviously. I had the presence of mind to say, 'This is not going to hurt me. Don't get scared. Just wait and see what's going to happen.' But unfortunately you would have seen me going, 'Aaahhh!'"

Many people have heard strange noises associated with paranormal events, and that seems to be true in this case. Jan was very impressed by the noise and was frustrated that she couldn't describe it to me. I asked her to try anyway. Says Jan, "Like a moaning. Not really like a human moaning, don't get me wrong. It was just like a moaning through the trees...it started out real low. And I think from the time it started until the point where it was real loud – and for us to be wandering through the house trying to figure out what the heck was going on – I would say it was at least a half an hour to forty-five minutes. It was just constant. I wish I had a tape recorder to tape it, because it was just a sensation. It was nothing I've ever heard before. My husband is, of course, the constant skeptic, and to tell you the truth, I never told him what was going on because he would have freaked out. And we'd have been gone. So I was just real quiet about it, as I related in the story. And Lisa didn't say anything. So consequently, Lisa and I had our experiences, but we never compared notes until after the fact. We kept checking water pipes. I mean, we did everything we could think of to figure out what this sound was. And then it just built to this crescendo, and then boom, it was gone. It was magnificent."

Jan also mentioned having had a few other encounters with the spirits of people she knew who had died. After her father died, she had many dreams of her father explaining to her what she should relate to her mother. And when her best friend's husband passed away, he came to her in her dreams and they had a long conversation that she was again supposed to relate to her best friend. She also had a friend on the east coast of the United States who committed suicide. When she went to visit the friend's family, she was standing in the kitchen and she felt the overwhelming presence of her friend.

Jan is a bit embarrassed by all of her experiences because she admits that she used to be largely skeptical of such stories, believing they were the result of overactive imaginations. It wasn't until she began having these experiences that she realized that ghosts were, in fact, very real indeed.

She also discovered that her family has a history of encountering ghosts. She learned that her grandfather was a talented medium, and that people who had died would manifest themselves to him as actual apparitions. Jan also learned that her aunt and uncle live in a haunted farmhouse in Minnesota. Somebody died in the house and the family has heard ghostly footsteps moving throughout the house. One night the parents were unable to open their bedroom door. There was no lock on the door and they were ready to actually chop it down with an axe when they tried to open it one more time, and it opened up easily.

For some yet unknown reason, ghostly encounters can be inherited. The ability to see ghosts runs in certain families. Jan Luber evidently inherited her ability to sense spirits from her grandfather. Jan feels lucky because her experiences have all been very positive. Although she was fearful in the beginning, she now takes her experiences in stride. She feels blessed and rightly so. Not everyone gets to feel what it's like to be hugged by the ghost of a sad wandering child in need of love.

# 6 – Only the Children

Like most ghost stories, this case begins with a tragedy. A North Holly-wood police officer was shot in the line of duty. He wasn't killed, but he became a paraplegic. After his recovery in the hospital, he returned to his home in North Hollywood. He was, of course, laid off from work. His only option was to stay at home and live on welfare and disability.

But evidently, the police officer was unable to recover emotionally from his accident. He became very depressed and was unable to resign himself to living the rest of his life in a wheelchair. One night in 1977, at what was later determined to be three a.m., the police officer placed a loaded gun to his head and pulled the trigger.

His body wasn't discovered until three or four weeks later. The police filled out a report. The cause of death was suicide.

The deceased police officer also left a will in which he gave the house to his mother-in-law. And so the story really begins.

Tracy Tyler (not her real name) is the lady who moved into the North Hollywood house. Tracy first began to suspect that something strange was happening when she was repeatedly woken up at exactly three a.m., night after night. She knew that the police officer had killed himself at that time and wondered if there was a connection.

She eventually learned to sleep the whole night through and would only be wakened periodically. But it was still always at the same time – three a.m., when the police said that the man had killed himself.

But then other mysterious events began to occur, such as unexplainable noises, as if someone was moving around in the house when she knew no-body was home. She would also hear things falling down, and when she went to check, nothing had fallen. But it wasn't until a very strange event occurred that everyone in the family could no longer deny that the house was haunted.

It was 1985, and five adults and three children were together in one of the bedrooms. They were all enjoying a relaxing evening when the youngest child, a girl of four years, began screaming in terror and pointing towards the entrance of the hallway. The little girl had been lying in bed when something in the hallway caught her eye. She sat up in fear, pointed at the doorway and began screaming, "There he is! There he is! The man!"

That was when things got really strange. Everybody looked at where the little girl pointed, however, nobody but her saw anything. Meanwhile, the girl was absolutely terrified.

One of the adults present was the godmother of the little girl. As she says, "My aunt lives in this house where this man killed himself, in the dining area place. And one night we were all there with my little goddaughter and we were laying in the bedroom. All of a sudden, she sat up in the bed and started screaming. 'There he is! There he is!' We looked and there was nobody there. She was screaming. I mean, there was nobody there and she kept on pointing in the hallway. She said it was a man. She says, 'There he is! There's a man!' And there was nobody there.

"My uncle kind of freaked out because he kept saying, 'There's nobody there! There's nobody there!' And she kept on saying, 'Yes, there's a man. There's a man!'

"They shut the door. You know, after you don't see anybody there and some little girl is screaming that there's somebody there, you've got the creeps and you shut the door...my aunt said it was the guy who killed himself.

"My goddaughter probably doesn't even remember it, but we were all freaked out. We were like, 'Stop it!'"

This case is very interesting because only the youngest child was able to see the ghost. To her the ghost appeared as an actual apparition of a man, but nobody else in the room saw anything. This sort of phenomenon, where only the children can perceive the ghost, is actually somewhat common.

One similar report comes from two young sisters. They were sleeping together in the same room. One night, in the middle of the night, they woke up because someone came into the room and sat down. Both of the girls sat up and saw very clearly who the person was. It was their aunt who had been dead for some time. Both the girls were extremely frightened and fled in terror to their parents' room. They told their parents what they saw and begged them to come and see. The parents went into the children's bedroom, but they could see anything. The two sisters, however, could still see their dead aunt very clearly sitting on a chair against the wall. The parents still couldn't see anything and accused the children of lying.

The two terrified girls were unable to convince their parents and were told to get back in bed and go to sleep. The two of them had no choice but to obey their parents. Eventually, they fell asleep. When they awoke the next morning, their aunt was gone.

Again, only the children could see the apparition and the adults were unable to see it. What could be the reason for this? One possibility could be the fact that children are open-minded and totally unprejudiced. They are very sensitive to their surroundings and carry no preconceptions about what they experience. Most paranormal researchers agree that children are often naturally psychic.

For whatever reason, as the above accounts prove, there are some ghosts that only children can see.

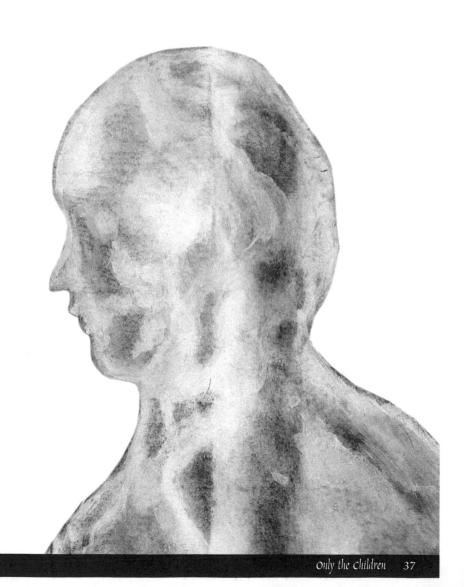

# 7 – Footsteps on the Staircase

If you've ever had anyone break into your house, you know it can be a very scary and upsetting experience. Then you can imagine how scary a phantom intruder would be.

There is a house in Canoga Park, a suburb of Los Angeles, California, that has been repeatedly entered by a ghost. Whenever anyone asks Dorothy Hudson if she's ever encountered a ghost, she says, "Oh, yes! God, yes!" For it is Dorothy's house that the ghost keeps coming back to, as if the ghost once lived there.

The family of four had no idea that their house was haunted when they moved in. It was a relatively new house, certainly not the type of place that would conjure up images of ghosts. It wasn't long, however, before each member of the household became convinced that something very peculiar was happening.

Each of them began to experience little events that seemed only slightly strange. Little odd things would happen that seemed to have no rational explanation. Someone would set a glass down on a table, turn away, and then find it mysteriously moved. Someone else would see a figure move in the back end of the house, only to look and find nobody there. Doors would be left open that they were sure they had closed, and lights would be left on that they were certain they had turned off.

At first, everybody kept the little events to themselves, passing them off as forgetfulness. Then, one by one, they would hear the front door open and close by itself, just as if somebody had come home. Except when they looked there was nobody there. Then they would hear footsteps walking up their staircase and nobody would be there.

All at once, all the pieces came together – the misplaced objects, the lights left on, the footsteps on the staircase. Dorothy and her family realized what was happening – they had a ghost!

And not only did they have a ghost, but it was a ghost that all of them had separately encountered. As Dorothy says, "I have witnesses. My ex-husband and my kids, we all lived in this big house. It was not an old house; it was just any new house up in Canoga Park. And all the time, we would see something moving. All of us had experiences many times. We'd see a shadow moving past us out of the corner of our eye, in one certain section of the house –

from upstairs, then it would move downstairs. Some of us, sometimes we'd be in the house and the front door would slam shut. We'd hear somebody walking up the steps. And then, all of a sudden, before they got to the top of the stairs, it would stop. I'd get up and I'd say, 'Who is that?' And I'd go down and there'd be nobody there. And all of us experienced that same thing: the front door slamming, somebody walking up the steps, and then nobody would be there. All of us.

"My daughter is standing here saying, 'I remember that.' It happened to her quite a few times too. Sometimes she'd be in the house alone, and she'd be scared to death because she'd hear the front door slam, and she'd hear somebody walking up the stairs. And then, all of a sudden, the footsteps would stop.

"Everyone would walk out and look, and there would be nobody there. And the front door slammed just as if ten people had walked in.

"Other strange things happened in that house. Certain things would be missing. I'd set something down and it would be moved to another side of the kitchen. Basically it happened in the stairway leading upstairs, the hallway, and in the kitchen. I never saw anything move, actually move from one side of the counter to the other. But I would put something in the kitchen, and I would come back later and it would be on the other side of the kitchen. And every one of us had experienced that too."

Dorothy said that the objects seemed to move as soon as she turned around, almost in a matter of seconds. It finally got to the point that she knew that something very strange was happening, that it wasn't just absent-mindedness.

Nobody in the family had any idea who the ghost could be. As far as they knew, nobody had ever died in the house. It was a large house, but they couldn't think of any reason that a ghost would be there.

But the ghost *was* there. Whether they liked it or not, Dorothy and her family learned to live with the ghost, simply because they had no choice. They couldn't stop the ghost from slamming door and picking up combs, ashtrays, pencils, and other small objects, and setting them down somewhere else.

Not only did they learn to live with the ghost, it got to the point where a self-closing door followed by phantom footsteps was no longer paranormal. It was normal.

The ghost became almost a member of the family, one that was perhaps blamed for more than its fair share of missing or misplaced objects. The children found it particularly convenient to have a ghost around to blame for the toy they had left in the middle of the hallway.

I know of a case very similar to this one, except that it took place in an apartment in Los Angeles. The man who lived there said that his roommate had been surprised many times when the front door opened and closed by itself, and footsteps moved through the living room. And when the roommate checked to see who was there, of course the apartment was empty.

They asked the landlord about the previous tenants and learned that an alcoholic man had lived there and that he had actually killed himself in the apartment.

The two men are convinced that their apartment is haunted by the spirit of the man who killed himself.

In these cases, it seems that the spirits are either attached to the home the used to live in, or are simply not aware that they are dead and are returning to their homes as would any living person.

So if you are ever interrupted by the sound of your front door opening and closing, and you hear footsteps moving through your house, and you check only to find your house empty, you'll know that you have a visitor in your house. A very special visitor. A ghost!

# 8 – A Vision of Blood

One of the most common type of ghost experience is known as a crisis apparition. The typical example of this type of ghost experience is when a person suddenly sees the ghost of a loved one, only to get a phone call a little while later, confirming that the loved one died at the same moment the person saw the apparition.

I know many people who have had varying degrees of this experience. Two of the cases involved ladies who were woken up out of a sound sleep to hear their mothers calling their names. The next morning, they both found out that their mothers had died during the night. A third case involves a lady who suddenly just *knew* that her sister had died. A short while later, a phone call confirmed that she was correct. Another young girl saw the ghost of her father at home, not knowing that he had just expired in the hospital a few miles away.

Many people receive subtle clues that somebody they know has died. Sometimes, however, the clues are not so subtle. In the following case, Dorothy Hudson received a dramatic clairvoyant vision that unfortunately turned out to be true. It was a crisis apparition of a very unusual sort. Dorothy was working in a business office in Los Angeles, California, when the experience occurred.

As she says, "One experience that I had was a very, very emotional experience. I was working with this woman that I did not get along with. She was a bill collector, and she was just an ugly person inside and out. And she and I had not an argument, but a disagreement. She left that day, and we were not speaking to each other.

"The next morning, she was supposed to go out to Titus Street in Van Nuys, to pick up a check that a person owed. They told her, 'You come out here and pick up this check,' which once in a while she did, but not very often.

"She was going to pick the check up at eight-thirty in the morning and be to work by nine. By nine-thirty she didn't come into work. And we didn't have a phone call from her, which we thought was a little strange.

"Around ten or ten-thirty, I went to the restroom. The ladies' restroom is all white. I walked into the restroom. And when I opened the door, I saw blood spattered all over the floor, all over the walls. And then that flash went away. It was a momentary thing. I said, 'Oh, my God! What the hell did that mean?'"

Dorothy just shook her head and tried to put the vision out of her mind. She told one of her co-workers who thought that it was not a good sign. Dorothy had already figured that much out, but she hadn't connected it to her co-worker who was inexplicably late. It wasn't until a few hours later that Dorothy found out what had caused her vision of blood.

As Dorothy says, "Around eleven o'clock, this woman – her name was Margery [pseudonym] – her husband called and asked, 'Is Margery there?'

"And I told him, 'No, she went out to Titus Street in Van Nuys this morning, to pick up a check. And she hasn't called or anything, and we don't know where she is.'

"He said, 'Oh, no! Oh, my God! No!'

"I said, 'What's wrong?'

"He said, 'I don't know…just got a call from the police. I'll call you later.'

"Well a couple of hours later he called up and said that after Margery picked up the check, she was jay-walking across the street to her car. A Mayflower moving van did not see her coming, backed up, knocked her down on the ground, and ran over and killed her.

"My boss went to her car, and he said that she was killed just a few feet from her car, that there was blood all over the street, all over the car, just blood every place. And that whole incident happened when I saw blood all over the bathroom. It happened approximately an hour after she was killed because she died at approximately nine to ten in the morning; it was ten o'clock went I went into the restroom, ten-fifteen.

"And I knew something was wrong someplace. There was a lot of blood. She was literally run over by this truck, a huge big Mayflower van. It was kind of traumatic for me to walk into a room and see blood spattered all over the walls.

"So it was just a flash. I came back in, and I told my boss's daughter. 'I just really had a bizarre thing happen. I just walked into the bathroom and I saw this.'

"She said, 'Oh, my God! Something's happened to somebody.'

"I said, 'I don't know.' But it never dawned on me that it would be Margery, someone that I immediately worked with. Or that it would happen within the hour that she died."

This case is a typical crisis apparition. What is unusual about this particular case is that Dorothy's connection with Margery was really only by acquaintance. And as Dorothy said, she and Margery did not even get along. It is strange that Dorothy would have a vision of her death.

The obvious conclusion from this is that Dorothy is probably psychic. Evidently it was her connection with Margery, as minor as it was, that allowed her to receive the vision. Certainly, many people are killed every year in Los Angeles alone, but Dorothy picked up only upon the one that affected her personally. Although Dorothy didn't actually see a ghost, what she saw was a very clear message that something terrible had happened.

# 9 – A Mentally Handicapped Ghost

This next case is a perfect example of how a haunting can start with a few minor incidents and then escalate into a full-blown paranormal infestation.

Arlene Sanchez, her husband, Louis, and their two children, Tina and Ramon, (pseudonyms) were overjoyed to be moving out of their old home and into a new one. Louis' parents had purchased another house next to their own in Santa Monica, California, and they told Louis and Arlene that they would give them a good deal on rent if they wanted to live there. Of course, they accepted the generous offer and began plans to move in.

Although the house was not brand new, it was fully-equipped with a modern kitchen and was also in a very good neighborhood. But best of all, Louis and Arlene could live next door to Louis' parents. It seemed like a dream come true.

One thing about the house, however, was odd right from the beginning. One of the rooms was fully equipped with a sprinkler system and padded walls. Louis asked his parents about the room, and they said that a young mentally handicapped boy had been kept in that room, and that it had been specially designed with his handicap in mind.

At the time, this didn't concern the Louis or Arlene in the least. Because this room was the largest and nicest room, Louis and Arlene decided that it would be their master bedroom. Their two children, Ramon, nineteen and his sister, Tina, twenty-one, each got their own room.

Everyone loved the house and the first few nights were spent peacefully. However, less than two weeks after they moved in, a strange incident occurred. The family of four was asleep, each in their own rooms, when a huge resounding crash reverberated throughout the house, waking everybody up. The sound had come from the bathroom. Everybody rushed in there together to see what could possibly have made so much noise.

Arlene was shocked at what she saw. Earlier she had bought two expensive ceramic ducks which she had placed on the shelves in the bathroom. When she rushed into the bathroom, she saw that these ducks had somehow both flown off the shelf and shattered. As Arlene says, "It was really strange because we heard a big noise in the middle of the night, and when we came to the bathroom to see what it was, the duckies had fallen to the floor, but the shelf hadn't. So we thought this was kind of strange, but we didn't think much about it."

In fact, they reasoned that the ducks must have somehow just slipped. Ghosts never entered their minds. But then other small unexplained incidents began to occur. Before long, other items and the ducks, which Arlene had painstakingly glued back together, flew off the shelves again. As Arlene says, "Lots of little things started happening similar to that, because it happened more than once. Then we started thinking twice about it. Again, the shelf in the bathroom – same thing. I had another shelf in the bathroom and I had some little knick-knacks there. And the things would fall off the shelf. It was really strange that the shelf would not fall off, just the items on top of them. So that's when we started to know it was kind of weird.

"The duckies fell off. They broke, and we put them back together again. And then they fell again! And that was the thing. There was the shelf sitting right there, and the ducks were on the floor. And it's like, 'Wait a minute! Now, how did this happen?!' And plus, the shelf is not thin. It's not a skinny little shelf. The duck – somebody had to have pushed it off. I mean, I have the same duck. It's been there for a long time. The other one broke real bad. They both cracked. These ducks cost me thirty-two dollars so I was so upset about my ducks.

"So then what happened was my husband glued them together and put them back up there. And the second time it happened again, and one was totally demolished. We saved the other one. I said, 'I am not giving up my duck!' So now I have the ducks and a bell up there, a little ducky-bell. But the shelf is kind of round, and you had to have gotten the duck and actually hit it with your hand. That type of thing."

What does a family do when their ceramic ducks fly across the room by themselves? Is there anything they can do? Louis and Arlene realized that something strange was occurring, but all they could do was try not to be afraid and see what happened next. The incidents with the ducks had happened in July 1991, soon after they moved in. Through the next three months, minor paranormal incidents began to occur throughout the house. They often seemed to involve electrical appliances. Lights, radios, and televisions began to turn on and off by themselves. Objects began to move by their own accord.

The next incident after the ducks involved the television. Tina and her aunt were watching TV. Tina hadn't told anybody what happened because she didn't think it was important. It was only when Arlene brought up the duck incident and insisted that it was unusual that Tina remembered what had happened to her and her aunt while watching TV late at night. As Arlene says, "They were watching TV, and they decided to turn off the television and put the remote control on top of the TV. Everything was off in the bedroom when, all of a sudden, the TV went back on. And we thought that was strange."

Despite the fact that televisions do not turn themselves on and off, Tina and her aunt just dismissed the incident, thinking only that it was a little strange. Certainly it wasn't spooky or even scary. None of them were even interested or curious about it. At least, not yet.

About a week or two later, the next incident occurred. The entire family was away from the house, and Louis' mother, who lived next door, went in the house and nobody was there. On Arlene's refrigerator are several large magnets used to hold paper notes. The magnets are quite large and are difficult to pull off the refrigerator. As Louis' mother walked through the house, she noticed that one of the magnets had popped off the refrigerator and flown eight feet across the room.

Arlene explains, "She came into our house. And she said when she was going back, what she thought was odd, she said that the magnet had fallen. But it wasn't right underneath the refrigerator. It was towards the door, maybe six or eight feet from the refrigerator, and some of the things it was holding were on the floor. But yet, she said there was no wind, no windows open, and when she came back she thought, 'How odd! Why is this magnet all the way over here?'

"And I still have the same magnets, and they're still on the refrigerator. And they don't fall off because they're big magnets. And it's the same magnet. So that was really strange that that would happen without any wind or any doors open at all."

Louis' mother had no idea at all about the other strange events that had been occurring in the home. All she knew was that the magnet had not been on the floor when she first walked in. Arlene hadn't mentioned anything because it hadn't quite clicked in her own mind that they had a ghost in the house. When Arlene heard about the occurrence, she just thought it was strange. She didn't really connect it with the ducks falling or the television turning on.

But then, another incident occurred in the middle of the night which brought it all together in her mind. She and Louis had been sleeping when they were woken up by a huge crashing noise in the living room. Their dog, Frosty, who sleeps on the floor next to their bed, began barking furiously. As soon as Arlene and Louis opened the door, Frosty bolted down the hallway to the living room towards the sound. Louis and Arlene were right on his heels. They all searched the living room and it appeared that nothing was out of order. They decided that the noise must have come from somewhere else. They calmed the dog down and went to sleep. It wasn't until the next morning that they saw what had happened. Someone or something had moved a piece of furniture across the room.

As Arlene says, "That was a really strange thing. We can't remember what that was, but it was so weird because we heard something in the middle of the night. Something was moving in the living room. And it's a pretty long hallway. I mean, if you're in the bedroom, it's hard to hear what going on in the living room because it's such a long hallway. There are two bedrooms in-between, and then a long hallway, and then our bedroom. But we heard something in the living room. And my husband, I grabbed him. It was in the middle of night. We heard something strange in the living room. My husband got up, but we just can't seem to remember. We just can't seem to remember what it was, but it was strange.

"Frosty also ran to the living room and barked. He was barking. He ran towards the hallway into the living room, because he felt the same thing that we heard. And he ran, and he was barking and barking into the living room and towards a window. And that's what made us even more suspicious, that Frosty felt something too that night – the same night we went into the living room, and I don't know what it was."

Although their dog, Frosty was a four-pound, hyperactive, little Maltese, they had never seen him react so strongly. And the next morning when they saw that things had been rearranged, they were convinced that something really strange was happening. For the first time they began to suspect that there was a ghost in their house.

By now it was October and the events were becoming more frequent. Tina had another experience, this time with the radio. Tina had turned it off, and right afterwards, it turned on by itself, just like the television had done. As Arlene says, "Tina was in her bedroom and the phone rang. And she couldn't hear because her radio was in the bedroom, and she told her boyfriend, 'I'm going to go in the kitchen. Let me turn off the radio in the bedroom.' So she turned off the radio in the bedroom, and she came into the kitchen. And then, all of a sudden, she started hearing noise – the rhythm of music. It was really strange because the music was back on the radio."

Tina was quite surprised that the radio had turned back on by itself. She was absolutely certain that she had turned it off. She remembered the incident with the television and figured that the two events were probably related. A mere three days later, Tina had another similar experience. As Arlene says, "Tina and her boyfriend were here by themselves on a Sunday evening, and we were gone for the day. They decided to go out for a hamburger and they turned on the light in the living room because it was already dark, and so that when they'd come back, they wouldn't trip. And when they came back, everything was pitch black."

Neither Tina nor her boyfriend were particularly frightened by the incident. They turned the light back on and searched the house. Of course, nobody else was in the house. Tina remembered the television and the radio. And now there was the light. All of their machines couldn't be breaking at once. Somebody was turning them on and off, somebody they couldn't see.

About a week later, in the beginning of November, the next incident occurred. Again it involved the television, but this time the witnesses were Louis and Arlene. As Arlene says, "Both my husband and I had the day off, and we were on the bed. He was reading the paper and I was watching television. All of a sudden, the television just turns off by itself. And my husband and I look at each other like, 'Wow! What's happening? Did you see that?' And he looks at me and just...one good thing about it, we are not really frightened. This doesn't frighten us. So we just thought since little things like that had been happening, we just looked at one another like, 'Whoops! There it goes again!'"

As happens to many people who live in a haunted house, the Sanchez's found that the paranormal was becoming normal. They were actually getting used to their ghost. Four months had passed since they had first moved in, and at least eight unexplained incidents had occurred. The ceramic ducks fell twice, the TV turned on, the magnet popped off, a noise was heard in the living room at night and objects were found moved in the morning, Frosty acted strangely, the radio turned on, and the light turned off.

Any one of the incidents occurring alone would mean nothing. But taken together, they were virtually impossible to explain as natural occurrences. Even if they had been explainable, Arlene was soon to have an experience that would leave her absolutely convinced that there was a ghost in their house. And she also had a pretty good idea who the ghost was.

The event occurred in the middle of the night, on the same day that the television had turned off by itself in the master bedroom. Arlene was asleep when she was woken up by the sound of footsteps moving through her room. The sound brought her wide awake and she was able to listen to the footsteps very clearly for several minutes. She was just beginning to fall back asleep when she heard the footsteps move to the side of her bed and a sudden noise blasted in her left ear.

As Arlene says, "It was really weird because it was about three o'clock in the morning and I was sound asleep. And I'm the type of person who sleeps through everything unless there's a big bang or something like that. I mean, knock out. I have no problems sleeping at all. I don't have to take anything to go to sleep, and I sleep my full hours.

"And it was really strange because it was about three o'clock in the morning, and I could feel something in the room. Everything in our house is carpeted except for the kitchen and our bedroom. Our bedroom is the only one that has hardwood floors. So I felt that there was something in the bedroom. And what woke me up was the sound of someone dragging their feet, like slippers, dragging your feet with slippers on. So the only place that those slippers could be heard if someone dragged their feet would be in our bedroom.

"I opened my eyes. I was wide awake, and I could hear these really soft footsteps, but somebody dragging their feet. So I looked over to see if my husband was in bed, and sure enough, he was sound asleep, breathing. And I made sure that it wasn't my dog shaking or scratching. My dog sleeps right next to me on the side, and he was sound asleep. And I kind of looked up and looked at the time.

"I stayed really still, and every once in a while you would hear these feet dragging. So I said, 'Oh, well. I'm not afraid.' It doesn't seem to scare us as far as nothing too spooky to want to harm us. So I just said to myself, 'I'm not afraid. It's three o'clock and I have to go to work, and I'm not going to worry about it.'

"So I was starting to doze off, and just as I was starting to doze off, right in my ear, there was this big humming sound. It was, hmmmmm. And I guess this thing, or spirit, or whatever it is, maybe it can't talk.

"And it was really strange because it came right into my ear and made this real humming sound. And I looked over and it wasn't my husband because he was sound asleep. And I still wasn't that asleep. I would have known if it had been him."

After Arlene heard the humming noise, she thought of the handicapped child who used to be kept locked up in the very room in which she was sleeping. She wondered if he used to shuffle through the room. She also had a strong feeling that he was unable to talk and could only make humming noises. She thought of the lights, radios, and television turning on and off and realized it would be just like a child to do something like that to get attention.

The incident with the humming changed Arlene. She was now absolutely sure that their house was haunted, and she was pretty sure that it was the ghost of the handicapped boy. She was intrigued and excited about the whole event, and vowed to find out if the boy had died in the house or was perhaps still living somewhere else.

She called the entire family together for a meeting to discuss their ghost. As Arlene says, "It's kind of a little joke now. We're open. We've talked to the kids about it. We are open about it because I don't want them to be frightened either. I don't want this to be a surprise. We've talked about the lights. We've talked about the radio, about the TV turning on and things like that, so that they're more aware. I don't want them to be frightened. But you know, kids are always jumping around and making noise. But once they're asleep, they're asleep. There's no noise here. And everything seems to be really peaceful after everybody's in bed. And that's when these incidents have happened – when everything's a lot quieter."

The entire Sanchez family became engaged in the mystery and adventure of having a ghost in their home. Arlene was unable to find out if the handicapped boy had died in the house or not. Being religious, she would frequently pray that the spirit would find peace. She holds no fear at all, and for a while, it seemed like the ghost went away.

Then Tina began having nightmares that an evil, black form was trying to suffocate her. She felt that it was the ghost and that it was evil. She also reported that she was eating with her friends in a fast food restaurant when she saw two glowing red lights, like eyes, staring at her from the next table. She thought she must be hallucinating, but the fear she felt was too familiar – it was the ghost.

Shortly later, the Sanchez family moved out of the Santa Monica home. Since then, they have had no experiences. The house was sold and they never contacted the new owners to find out if they also were experiencing activity. They were happy to leave the house and all their experiences behind. Tina, especially, was uncomfortable with the ghost. She would be happy to never encounter another ghost.

Arlene, on the other hand, was never frightened by the events that occurred in her home. She neither desires nor fears any new experiences. To her, having a ghost in your house is a situation to be dealt with like any other situation, with patience and understanding.

# 10 – The White Witch

There are literally thousands of hauntings taking place across the world. These include hauntings of many kinds, from simple apparitions to poltergeist infestations, nature spirits, possession cases and many others.

Some hauntings have become very well known because of their faithful and constant manifestations of paranormal events. Places like Hearst Castle or the Queen Mary produce ghost reports on a regular basis.

Another very famous haunting is currently taking place in a small community in El Sobrante, California. It remains one of the most widely experienced and bizarre hauntings on record. Many people in the area consider it to be a living legend.

The haunting is unique in that it centers around the ghost of an old woman who has a voracious appetite for young, blond men. The story is well known in the area and many of the local residents have good reason to believe that it is more than just a legend. The reason for this is because some of them have encountered this "legend" face-to-face.

As the story goes, over a hundred years ago in the foothills of El Sobrante, there lived an old lady who had a reputation for being a witch. Many people believed she practiced black magic and dabbled in other areas most people shy away from. The old lady's downfall, however, was her young, beautiful daughter who had just reached dating age.

The daughter, naturally, longed for male companionship. And one night the daughter brought home a handsome, young, blond sailor. All three spent the evening in the small cottage owned by the old lady.

In the middle of the night, a fire was somehow ignited. The sailor was able to escape the house safely, however the old lady and her daughter weren't so lucky. Both of them were trapped in the house and died in the blaze.

Ever since that evening, people have reportedly seen the ghost of the old woman traveling along the roads, looking for the blond sailor who left both her and her daughter to die. She appears in flowing white garments, and floats a few feet above the ground. She is tall and slender and glows brightly enough to cast a considerable amount of light. According to the legend, more than one young, blond man has been mistaken for the amorous sailor and was attacked by the ghost of the old lady.

Today the ghost is popularly known as the White Witch. A full-length book has been written about the legend and can be found in the El Sobrante Library. The legend has gained such a solid reputation for a very good reason. There are many, many witnesses who have seen the White Witch, including several modern-day accounts.

One famous account is that of two ladies who were riding horseback on the back roads of the foothills when they encountered the White Witch. According to their testimonies, they were riding peacefully when they heard a noise behind them. They turned around and saw the tall, white form of the ghost hovering behind them. The two women were instantly terrified and took off at a gallop. To their surprise, the ghost easily kept up with them. They slowed down and the ghost slowed down. They sped up and the ghost again matched their speed. After a long, hair-raising gallop that went on for several minutes, the ghost stopped the chase. The two ladies, however, decided that it was in their best interest to keep running away.

Some of the other accounts are even more bizarre. For example, several independent witnesses have reported seeing the ghost riding on the backs of cows!

Despite these encounters and others, many of the local residents find the stories a little hard to believe. An evil witch who loves blond boys and rides cows? It all seemed too much like a bad movie. Or so thought five young men, all residents of El Sobrante.

The five young men are members of a heavy metal rock band, ranging in age from late teens to early twenties. One summer evening in 1990, they were searching for inspirations to write some new songs. That is when somebody brought up the legend of the White Witch.

None of them really believed the accounts, though part of them wondered if it could be true, if the White Witch was actually real. Then one of them got the idea to go on an impromptu ghost hunt. They kicked the idea around and being young and brave, and even more importantly, skeptical, they decided to give it a chance.

By coincidence, one of the witnesses, John H., has blond hair, so he was unanimously elected to act as bait for the ghost. The five of them waited until past midnight, when the ghost was supposed to appear. Then they piled into their truck and set off towards Alvarado Park, which was said to be the area where the ghost had appeared many times before.

None of them really expected their idea to work. They were more curious and playful about the idea. They weren't really seriously expecting to see a ghost. So they were not at all prepared for what was about to happen.

They pulled up to the park, got out of the truck, and hiked up to a bench near the center of the park. They sat there for about fifteen minutes and just as they expected, there was no ghost. Disappointed, but not surprised, they decided to leave. They all stood up and began walking. It was at that exact moment that the White Witch made her dramatic appearance. All at once, there was total panic.

As John, the bait for the ghost, says, "We started walking up the path to go back up towards the truck, and [the White Witch] started walking up on us, and everybody started racing for the truck. Our ex-drummer turned around and looked, and then we all looked, and it was like, 'Aaahhh!' and we ran."

As they ran, the ghost chased them a mere ten feet behind. One of the witnesses, Tom X., remembers the incident vividly. As he says, "We were just ready to leave the place when she came out and started coming towards us. So we kind of split real quick...we saw her and then she started coming towards us, and we kind of bugged."

The ghost was so close, the witnesses couldn't help but get a clear view of her. As Tom says, "She was white and she was pretty tall. She was almost six feet, and she kind of hovered above the ground. There were no feet, just her and her dress following behind her. Really trippy. I was kind of worried about getting out of there."

Despite the close proximity of the ghost, some of the witnesses admit that they were too frightened to carefully observe the ghost. As John says, "All I really saw was a big, white flash because I turned, looked, and ran."

The three others report the same details, but it was Tom who got the clearest view. Says Tom, "You could kind of see through her, especially at the end of her dress. She put off a pretty bright glow."

All five of the witnesses ran screaming towards the truck. As soon as they reached it, they piled in and raced away, not even daring to look back. All of them admit that the experience scared them badly.

After a few minutes of racing down the narrow streets at top speeds, they finally stopped the truck and began discussing what they had just seen. There was no doubt in any of their minds what it was. They had just encountered the infamous White Witch in all her blaze and glory.

None of them could believe it was true, but their sweaty palms and beating hearts betrayed them. They were *scared*. And yet, they were still suspicious. Had they *really* encountered the White Witch? Could it really be *that* easy?

None of them wanted to admit to each other that they were actually scared, and peer pressure being the incredibly strong force that it is, the four boys soon found themselves deciding to head back deeper into the area to see if they could provoke the ghost into another appearance.

Despite the fact that none of them really wanted to see the ghost again, they turned the truck around and drove back to Alvarado Park where they had just encountered the ghost. This time they decided to play it safe and stay in the car. It wasn't long before they got the confirmation they were look-ing for. The White Witch appeared without warning, and again, the experi-ence proved more terrifying than they expected.

As they sat in the truck the ghost began appearing and disappearing all around them. There was no doubt that the ghost knew exactly where they were and was either trying to scare them or was getting ready to attack them. Only then did they realized that they were probably dealing with something more powerful and unpredictable than they had bargained for.

At that point, the young men's priorities promptly changed. Ghost-hunt-ing suddenly lost its charm and the only thing the witnesses cared about was leaving the area as quickly as possible. As Tom says, "We went deeper into the park, kind of where – I don't know if it's true – where she always hangs out. We stayed there a long time. It took us a long time to get this close by, but we took a detour road. Then we were resting up and she came out again. She appeared and disappeared, then appeared somewhere else...we saw her a couple of times."

This time, John, who was no longer comfortable being used as bait for the ghost, got a slightly better view of the White Witch. As he says, "We went to Tilden Park and we were kicking back in the car watching the stars and stuff. And we started hearing these dogs barking. So we started looking and she came out of the bush. We left. We didn't stop to look at her. She was just a white woman with a long white dress. I didn't really look at her very well."

Just like the first time, they again started the car and raced away as fast as they could. John, however, kept his eye on the ghost and was able to make out more details. According to John, the she was extremely bright and very physical-looking. As he says, "She was pretty solid, really bright. As long as we drove away, I kept my eye on her...we had a lot of people with us who saw it. We all saw it."

By this time, the young men were sufficiently convinced of the White Witch's existence. All their desires to continue their ghost hunting had van-ished, never to return. Simply put, the White Witch was too mean and too scary.

They all rushed home to their friends and family and told their story. One of their friends verified that they were all very excited and were obviously telling the truth. She clearly remembers how scared they all were as they explained what had happened. As hard as it was to accept that the White Witch was real and that her friends had encountered her, she found herself unable to disbelieve them.

John's older sister also verified their story and even recalled new details. As she says, "My dad wasn't there so I didn't go along. I didn't feel like being hunted. They used my brother for bait because he's blond, and it worked! When the boys went out there, they said that they saw her in three different parks. They saw her five times. One of the times, she actually split up into five different people, because there were five guys that went, and they were going, 'She's over here! No, she's over here! No, she's over here!' And they were all right!"

A large number of people have vouched for the honesty and integrity of the various witnesses. There is little doubt that the incident happened as described. And as such, it represents an event which may be unique in the history of ghostly phenomena. In essence, five people were able to invoke a ghost into appearing using the simple knowledge that the ghost has a reputation for attacking young, blond men. They set up bait and to their surprise, it worked. They were able to provoke the ghost into appearing at least twice.

As it turns out, this ghost is particularly active. Like many ghosts, the White Witch has a purpose. She is fixed on the idea of avenging her daughter. And like most ghosts, she probably does not know that she is dead. Her focus on revenge has blinded her to the reality of her situation. And until she is somehow released from her torment, the White Witch will continue to appear.

She is now one of the most famous ghosts in California. Nearly everybody in the El Sobrante area knows about her and many have seen her. The five witnesses who encountered the White Witch will never forget what they saw on that summer night in 1990.

Needless to say, they all now believe in ghosts.

# 11 – So You Don't Believe in Ghosts?

Despite the fact that there are thousands of ghosts accounts going back to the dawn of history, there are many people who still don't believe in ghosts.

All it takes to believe in ghosts, however, is to see one. Unfortunately, most of us don't have the opportunity to simply go and see a ghost. And so we remain comfortable in our belief that ghosts don't exist.

Karen S., of North Hollywood, California, never really gave much thought to ghosts. Then, in the late 1970s, she went to visit her uncle in England. While she was there, she made the mistake of revealing to him that she didn't believe in ghosts.

Her uncle not only believed in ghosts, he knew where some ghosts were. And when he discovered that his niece was a skeptic, he decided to take her to visit a few of his favorite haunts. On the agenda were a haunted monastery, a haunted hangman's block, and a ghostly horse.

Karen's uncle was a little on the eccentric side. So when he promised to show her some ghosts, she didn't really take him seriously. She had no idea that he was totally serious and that she would soon be encountering things she had never even dreamed existed. It was to be an experience that Karen would never forget. Especially because, ever since that day, Karen has continued to see ghosts wherever she goes.

As she says, "What really triggered everything is when we went to England for a couple of months. And in England, everyone thinks that ghosts are the matter of the day. My mom lived in a town from the thirteenth century. There was a haunted monastery...we saw haunted monks in the monastery. They were brown hooded figures walking. I was so scared. I was seventeen. It was daytime. My uncle was a bit drunk and he's going, 'Look! Look over there, Karen. It's bloody right in front of you!' And they were there, just standing. I remember there were a number of them at this monastery when we were in the town.

"They walked down this little hall. It was all full of nettles. It was a broken-down monastery where supposedly monks had tortured people. And there were a number of them just filing, like they all had a journey...I don't really remember too much because I was so scared. I said, "Okay, that's enough!' And we left."

Karen's uncle, however, had only just begun. If Karen didn't believe in ghosts yet, she would after the next visit. Karen's uncle took her to a place known as Hangman's Lane, so named because it was the previous location of many executions by hanging. To this day, the sound of the noose being drawn can still be heard.

Karen, of course, was skeptical. She soon had reason to change her mind. As she says, "Then we went down to Hangman's Lane, and we heard the noose. All you heard was a 'Sssshhhkkk! Creeakkk!' And he said, 'That's the sound of the hangman.' It was just there."

Karen was stunned by the noise. She had no idea that ghosts could be so active. After Hangman's Lane, she had to admit that she was pretty much convinced that ghosts were real. However, her uncle wasn't through with her yet.

He decided to show her another famous ghost known locally as "the charging horse." As Karen says, "Then we went to this one house where this man supposedly loved his horse so much that he had his horse buried with him. And there was this thing that you saw. It was like a white, blurry thing with silver hooves that charged by you and went down the lane where this old mansion used to be. And there it was. I saw something. It looked kind of like the shape of a horse, but just the shape in front, and charging legs, and all this dust. And it was more like you really didn't see an actual horse. And you didn't see a saddle. It was more like just a shape – a white shape."

After the last experience, Karen begged her uncle to stop. She believed in ghosts. Her uncle acquiesced and promised to stop taking her to haunted places and scaring the wits out of her.

England, however, is a very ancient country. Many of the structures and towns go back centuries. Ghosts are the matter of the day for a very good reason – so many people have seen them. In fact, it can actually be more difficult to avoid seeing ghosts than trying to see one.

Karen found this out the hard way. A short time later, she was to have another encounter with a ghost. She went to visit a distantly related cousin who, as luck would have it, just happened to live in a haunted house.

At the time of the visit, Karen was trying her best not to think of ghosts. And of course, she had no idea that she was visiting yet another haunted house.

As she says, "I went to his house, and he lived in a gatekeeper's house. And he went to the store, and I was at his house. It was two levels and I was upstairs. And I heard somebody go clunk-clunk-clunk-creak, and open the door. I looked over and there was nobody there. The bedroom door opened, and I said, 'Hello?' And there was nobody there! So I'm starting to get the willies. I'm starting to go 'la-la-la-la-la-la' down the stairs, and I'm looking out the window hoping that he's going to come back soon. I had gotten a glass of milk or something, and all of a sudden, I turned around and it moved across the table and whoosh! And it broke!"

Karen stared at the glass in amazement and fear. By now, however, she was beginning to get used to encountering ghosts. She simply waited patiently but vigilantly for her cousin to return home. When he finally arrived, Karen wondered if she should even tell him about the ghost. Maybe it was just her? After all, she had seen so many ghosts already. Maybe, she thought, it was affecting her mind.

As Karen says, "When he came in, I didn't say anything because, what am I going to say? And so what happened was, we started talking, and then he said, 'Oh, by the way, love, I just forget to tell you. I've got a friendly ghost here. He leaves things on the table, and he walks up and down the stairs, and he opens and closes the doors.' And I'm like, 'Shew! I'm so glad!'"

After that incident, Karen could honestly say that she had no doubts that ghosts were real. She definitely believed in ghosts. After the haunted monastery, Hangman's Lane, the charging horse, and now her cousin's friendly ghost, there was no way she could not believe. She learned the hard way that ghosts are real.

But there was also something else she learned. She discovered that she didn't like ghosts. They were too scary. She couldn't wait to get back to California, where ghosts don't pop out from behind every corner.

When she returned back to her North Hollywood home, however, she was in for an enormous shock. To her horror and disbelief, she discovered that her experiences in England had somehow given her or sparked within her the ability to see ghosts. Unknown to her, Karen was a medium.

One of her first ordeals back home was with a ghost that insisted on watching her get undressed as she readied herself for bed. As Karen says, "There were two ghosts that lived in the house. It was four houses down from the Shadow Hill Cemetery. I remember there was this liver-spotted man and he was mean. He was mean, wrinkly, and short. He had a Colonel Sanders bow-tie, and he was always wringing his hands. He did not have very good teeth.

"He lived in my bedroom. I would go to sleep at night and he would come and he would just stand there. He'd have these beady eyes and stare at me. And he was always there when I was undressing, getting ready for bed. That's when I'd see him."

Karen also began to see ghosts at her friends' houses. In 1976, she spent the night in her friends' old boarding house in Hollywood, California. At the time, she didn't know the house was haunted. As she says, "I spent the night at their house and I went downstairs to get a drink of water from the kitchen.

And they had a stair, an area that you turn into, and there was this big, blue cloud. It was sparkly stuff. And it was just there, and in the shape of a person. It was just a thing, a mass of energy. And I decided, 'I'm not going to walk through it.' And I walked back up and went to bed."

Karen later found out that there were four other witnesses to the same ghost. She also discovered on later visits that the building had another ghost – an old lady in a rocking chair. As Karen says, "The old lady in the rocking chair was in the same house. And it was in Hollywood. It was a Harvard House is what we called it. And she [the lady] was rocking. She must have been the caretaker. She was the caretaker. She didn't seem mad or anything. She looked solid."

On another occasion, Karen showed up a friend's new house that they were renting. She knew instantly that the house was haunted. As she says, "There are some houses that I can tell right away. I mean, one time I went to my friends' house when they rented a house. And they said, 'Oh, this house is really cheap.'

"And I'm saying, 'Wow, this is a bitchen house.' And I walked into the bedroom and said, 'Oh, my god! Who died here?! Did somebody get killed?'

"And my friend who rented the house said, 'Oh, my god! How did you know?' They had rented the house cheap because someone got killed in their bedroom. I walked in and I knew it."

Karen next found herself dealing with ghosts not only at her friends' house, but also at her work in Van Nuys, California! As Karen says, "I used to work over at Laser Images. I used to work at night by myself. And I have a friend there who believes in ghosts. And one night, we both noticed that there was somebody walking by.

"And what happened was, I'd be there at night alone, and it would always come around twelve o'clock. And I used to see somebody out of the periphery of my eye come from down the hall. And they would always just walk past, walk past. And I kept seeing a black-haired thing with a yellow fringe skirt walk by, walk by. And then if I got scared and I turned around and looked, it would stop and back up and it would just be there. And it would stay by the door and peek in and out.

"So I used to get spooked. I mean, I got spooked! And every time I got spooked, it would be there more. So finally, after a while, I realized what I was seeing. It was an Indian. It was a girl, an Indian woman with long, black braids. And it was not a yellow skirt. It was a buckskin dress with a fringe at the bottom. And the minute I turned around and looked, I said, 'Oh, it's you. I'm not afraid of you. I know who you are.' I never got scared anymore. It would just walk by. But every night, it was like she was always carrying something."

After facing the ghost, Karen found that the haunting became much less active. It used to happen at least twice a week. After she confronted it, it occurred only rarely. As Karen says, "I never saw her face. I just started to identify certain parts that I put together. And the minute that I put together that it was an Indian woman, it was like it had no fun with me. It was like it stopped coming. I think that the Indian girl had some trail past there. In my mind, she didn't know she was dead. She was just doing some natural walk of gathering water, or taking something. I just didn't know. She just kept going from place to place."

Karen also noticed that the ghost would become more active if she paid attention to it. As Karen says, "When I got spooked, it would stay longer. She would be there more when I was scared. A couple of times, I'd turn around and tell her, 'I'm not scared anymore. I know who you are.' And I wasn't scared, and she was gone."

Karen reports that at least two other employees at Laser Images also reported ghostly phenomena. Unknown to any of them, the San Fernando Valley was the location of a numerous Native American tribes. What is now dense city was once a fertile wilderness abundant with deer, bear, coyotes, cougars, beavers, rabbits, and countless other wild creatures. And the entire area was populated by thousands of Native Americans.

By now, Karen had seen so many ghosts that it had become something she began to expect. Not surprisingly, she continued to encounter ghosts. In 1987, Karen had yet another bizarre ghostly experience. It proved to her again that no matter where she goes, she is bound to encounter ghosts. Her latest experience again occurred in the San Fernando Valley. Not surprisingly, it also involved the ghosts of Native Americans.

As Karen says, "I moved into this new house and I kept waking up in the middle of the night because someone was playing this loud music. And I kept asking my roommates, 'Did you hear that last night? Did that wake you? What are they doing?'

"And they're saying, 'What are you talking about, Karen?'

"And I said, 'And what kind of music is that?' And then, after about two weeks of being there, it didn't happen anymore. So my friend had this book, *Haunted Places*, and supposedly right on our street, Sierra Bonita and Willoughby, there used to be a path where the Indians used to wait as the stagecoach passed. They would be there and wait for a raid, and then jump the stagecoach. And people have seen tomahawks flying and heard loud Indian music playing. And that's what it was. And he says, 'Oh, yeah!' Because I kept telling him, 'You won't believe these neighbors.' So I was looking at this book, and I said, 'Oh, I live in Hollywood.' And zoom-zoom-zoom, Sierra Bonita and Willoughby. And they said loud music had been heard by a number of people."

When asked to describe the music, Karen said it sounded like "nothing I've ever heard, like 'woo-woo-woo-woo.' At first I thought it was rap-ghetto music. There were drums."

Once again, Karen realized that she was encountering ghostly activity. She realizes now, of course, that she is psychic. But she prefers not to make a big deal about it. She doesn't like to see ghosts and has no desire to become a medium. As she says, "I think I have been put on this earth to deal with this now. I'm just too young. I have to be here to learn what's here now. But not now – it's just for me to know. I'll find out. Death is just like life, but different. All these people, 'Let's go find out about ghosts!' I'll be in that ghostly era soon enough as it is. You have to be here first. And if I start jumping into stuff like that...say I try to conjure up ghosts or I start looking for them? I don't want to see that. I don't want to see that dirty old man anymore."

Although she tries not to look for ghosts, Karen continues to encounter them. She also reports having a number of other psychic experiences. She has had many precognitive dreams and premonitions predicting earthquakes, car accidents, marriages, pregnancies, and other profound events.

Karen doesn't know why she had these experiences, only that she does. Although she doesn't enjoy seeing ghosts, she had learned to live with them as best as possible. Just as long as she doesn't let herself get too scared, she's fine.

There have been some advantages. Having had so many encounters with the unknown has taught her several things. Despite what anybody may say, she knows from personal experience that ghosts are very real indeed. She knows that there is life after death. And she knows that there are some things we just don't understand.

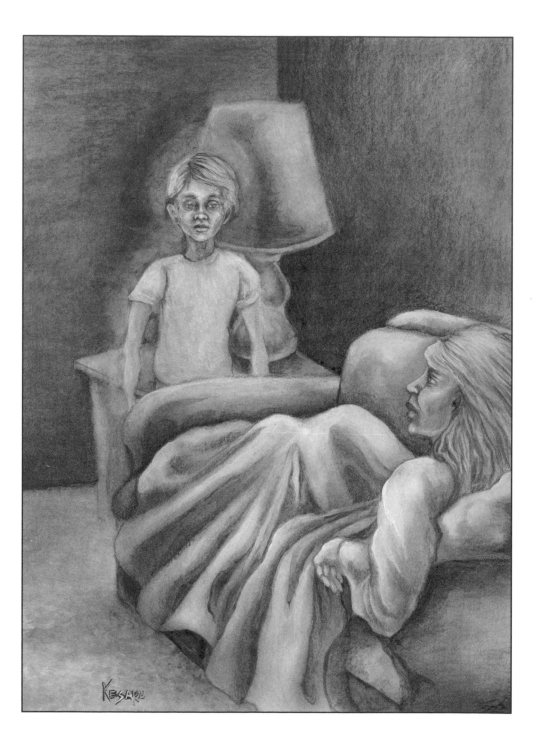

# 12 – A Child Ghost

There are as many kinds of ghosts as there are people. This allows for a great variety of apparitions to appear. As a general rule, ghosts are the result of a tragic or sudden death. Most people who die make a smooth transition to the higher dimensions. But a sudden and unexpected passing can create some problems. Most paranormal investigators agree that most ghosts are simply the spirits of deceased people. While some come with a purpose or a message, probably the majority of ghosts do not know that they are dead.

Therefore, whenever someone encounters a ghost, they are usually (but not always!) interacting with an entity that is confused, lost, or obsessed with the material world.

In the following case, the ghost of very young child haunted a young lady. In this case, the ghost appeared to be fixated in an emotional state of intense grief.

Deborah Danning (not her real name) lives with her parents and brother in a small home in San Francisco, California. She enjoys raising animals, listening to music, and reading lots of books. In most ways, Deborah lives the normal live of an eighteen-year-old woman.

There is one thing, however, that makes Deborah's life a little different. Her bedroom is haunted by the ghost of a lost little boy. At the age of fourteen, Deborah suddenly and for no apparent reason, became the focus of a dramatic haunting.

As Deborah says, "Well, my ghost is a kid, probably about six years old. He's got light brown hair. Now, I used to have a bed that was elevated off the ground because it had a wood bottom – it had wood underneath it. And I'd listen to the radio when I went to sleep, and I used to listen to country western music. And one night I was in bed sleeping and I heard this knocking underneath my bed in time to the music. And it scared me! So I grabbed my pillows and ran into the other room and went to sleep on the couch. You know, anywhere but in my room. And after about ten minutes of laying there with my eyes closed, I felt somebody watching me. So I opened my eyes and there's this kid standing at my feet. And I'm like, 'Oh!'"

Deborah was surprised to discover how frightened she was. Even though the little boy looked totally solid, Deborah had no doubt that she was seeing a ghost. He was looking straight at her. Deborah shook with fear and closed her eyes tightly, pulling the blanket over her head. She refused to look again and just waited for the ghost to go away. After a long while, she finally fell asleep.

At first, she thought it was freak event, something that would only happen once and never again. She had no idea that it was just the beginning of a long drawn-out haunting that would last for years. For some reason, the ghost of the little boy was drawn to Deborah and began appearing to her on a regular basis.

It was always the same routine. Deborah would be in her bedroom late at night. Suddenly she would hear a strange knocking sound. Usually she just went out into the living room and tried to sleep on the couch. But no matter where she chose to sleep, the ghost of the little boy would appear at the foot of her bed. Sometimes it would appear late at night, and Deborah was simply too tired to pay much attention. She would wake up on the living room couch and realize that the ghost must have come in the night, although she had no memory of it. As Deborah says, "The same thing, and it would be there. I didn't always remember that I had seen it. I'm one of those people that can wake up from a dead sleep and never remember anything. So I didn't always remember that it was there – he was there. And that happened over and over again for about a year."

Shortly after the haunting began, Deborah told her family and friends. Most of them believed her and understood her fear, but they had no idea what to do. As Deborah says, "I told people about it, and they said, 'Well, why don't you just ask it what it wants?' And I would tell myself, 'Okay, tonight I'm going to go out there, and I'm going to ask it what it wants.' And then I would open my eyes – there it would be. And I'd go, 'Oh, my God!' And I'd close them again real quick."

The haunting soon developed into a bizarre game of "Now you see me! Now you don't!" The ghost would appear to Deborah. She would close her eyes and wait for the ghost to go away. Usually, it would just disappear, but as Deborah says, "Sometimes he would still be there when I opened them...I could feel his stare is how I woke up. He was kind of standing there, looking at me, and I was like, 'Oh!'"

The little boy became something of an enigma. Nobody seemed to know who he was. As far as Deborah knew, nobody had ever died in the house. Actually, the location of their house used to be a river, but a large dam was constructed, making room for housing developments.

Eventually, the apparition stopped appearing. His expression, however, will always remain a haunting image in Deborah's mind. As she says, "He looked sad, very lost, very forlorn."

After the ghost stopped appearing, Deborah thought that the haunting was over. However, the household soon became plagued by other unexplainable events. Many small household objects mysteriously disappeared only to reappear in odd places throughout the house. Many of the objects were lost forever. As Deborah says, "It's very strange because you know that you could never lose something that thoroughly, that it would never turn up."

Another strange phenomenon that occurred intermittently was floorboards that would creak by themselves, just as if somebody was walking on them. This happened several times in full view of multiple witnesses, and yet, there was nobody there to make the noise.

Deborah explains, "It usually happens when you're alone and downstairs. Our house is pretty old. It has creaky boards. When you step on them, they creak. But it's only when you step on them. It's not like a house-creaky thing. It's just when you step on them.

"And there have been times when I've been alone, or my brother's been alone, or we've been together and no one else has been in the house, and then we'll hear it and it's just creaking. My mom's room is right above the living room, so her room is the one where it creaks. And you can hear the trail as it goes around the bed out in the hallway...it's very strange."

In 1990, Deborah had another unexplainable experience, though she is not sure if it was the ghost. As she says, "I didn't hear from him for years, and then the other night, a couple of months ago, I went to sleep listening to pop music and woke up listening to country music, with different channels. One was FM, and one was AM. So I don't know if it was him or if something decided to change the channels."

For the most part, the haunting has stopped. Deborah and her brother still hear the strange creaking noises every now and then, just as if someone was walking. But there have been no more apparitions.

Deborah admits that she was extremely relieved when the apparitions stopped manifesting. Waking up to see a ghost staring at you can be a little disconcerting. Although it scares her, Deborah does not feel that the ghost is evil. In her opinion, he was just a lost, little boy who was very, very lonely and just wanted some attention.

# 13 – Poltergeist!

Generally speaking, most ghosts originate with the spirit of a person who has died. However, some ghosts may have a different explanation.

Poltergeists are different from normal ghosts in that they are much more active. Poltergeist is German for "noisy ghost." These hauntings often have a huge variety of paranormal activity. Knockings, objects moving by themselves, electrical problems, apparitions, cold spots – all are just a few of the many ways a poltergeist makes itself known.

The cause of poltergeist hauntings is a hotly contested issue, though there are three main theories. The first theory is that poltergeists are caused by uncontrolled psychokinesis coming from a living person, often a pubescent teenager, who has repressed and dissociated their emotions and feelings. This theory says that poltergeists are internally generated and that the poltergeist is really just a burst of negative energy that an individual has subconsciously repressed and denied.

The second major theory is that poltergeists are demonic or diabolical in origin. This theory states that poltergeists are really an external evil force that is obsessed with hatred for humanity and God.

The third major theory is that poltergeist activity is the result of uncontrolled mediumship.

Poltergeists can be merely mischievous, or they can be downright dangerous. This seems to vary from case to case.

In the following case, a family lived with a poltergeist for many years. For them the activity was extremely mischievous. The haunting was very powerful, however, and was also experienced by the neighbors across the street.

The house is located in Northridge, California. The Johnson family had four members, the father and mother and two children, a boy and a girl. They lived in the house for many years with no problems. George Johnson was around fourteen or fifteen years old when the poltergeist suddenly became active.

It soon became apparent that the haunting was centered around George. The poltergeist would always come around late at night when he was alone in the house. Then it would do its very best to scare the wits out of him.

George describes what happened, "There was a lot of weird stuff that used to happen…one time I came home and there was nobody home and it was dark. And I turned on the light of the bathroom and it didn't go on. I walked back out to the kitchen and the light of the bathroom went on. And I walked back in and it went off again. And this went on for a few minutes and then the windows all rattled in the house, going around in circles, once in the front, then the side, then the back – I mean, rattled hard, like earthquake hard."

The poltergeist found other creative ways to express itself. Mostly, however, it continued to bother George. As he says, "Our house had a lot of mischievous stuff. It was really common that things would be unplugged, that appliances would come unplugged and in some places that you couldn't reach or it was difficult to reach. I remember the windows and the doors rattling on several occasions. I mean, the sliding glass door on the back would be rattling so violently and nothing else would be rattling. It was almost falling out of the track. And then another window would rattle in the back bedroom to the point of almost breaking.

"There was never any pattern that I could remember. They'd catch me at home and it would piss me off. I'd say, 'Go away! I'm the only one at home. Go haunt somebody else!' I remember always yelling at them, like, 'Cut this shit out! I'm not in the mood for it.' But they never bothered me or scared me. It would just be irritating. Once with the lights is fine. Twice is okay. Three, it's annoying. Cool it!"

The Johnson family was the proud owner of both a dog and a cat. Animals are well-known for being able to sense a ghostly presence, and that is certainly true in this case. Whenever activity would occur, the dog and cat would stare right at it and howl. As George says, "That was so common. I don't remember the particular time, but there would be different times that the dog and the cat would be staring at the top of the fireplace and just going crazy. The fur would be standing up on their backs and they'd be howling or hissing. That was pretty common. They would do that about a couple of times a month."

Poltergeists are well-known for expressing themselves in highly unusual ways. One uncommon manifestation that is nevertheless consistently reported is so bizarre, that it would be nearly impossible to make up. As George says, "I remember another night coming home and turning on the water in the kitchen and it came out of the faucet and went sideways like somebody had put their hand under it."

Another strange manifestation was the appearance of ghostly animals running through the house. As George says, "There were spirits of animals that would be running around every once in a while. That was pretty common, the animals running around the house. I don't remember seeing anything else in that house other than animals roaming around, little ghostly animals. They were kind of wispy. You knew what they were, but they were kind of in and out. I do remember that."

George told his family and they did believe him, however, they weren't sure how to react. They hadn't experienced much activity, nothing like George had. His sister was aware of some of the activity, but she and George never talked about it.

George, however, continued to have experiences. It got to be so common that he learned to just live with it. It never really scared him simply because he was so used to it. In fact, he would sometimes invite over his friends to see the activity.

One of the witnesses to this poltergeist is teacher and artist, Christine Dennett. When she was a teen-ager, her friend George would often talk about the fact that his house was haunted by a poltergeist. One day when Christine was visiting, the activity was going full tilt. Christine literally could not believe her eyes. As she says, "I had a friend who had a poltergeist, and I saw his poltergeist. He brought us in the living room and said, 'You want to see the poltergeist?'

"We said, 'Yeah.' I walked into the living room and there was a fireplace, a cat and a dog standing in front of the fireplace, two pictures framed above the awning of the fireplace. The dog was growling and barking, and the cat was hissing with all his fur up. You know, it was classic – looking up at the pictures and the pictures were sliding back and forth.

"He said, 'See, those are poltergeists.'

"And we said, 'Wow, that's really weird.' And then we left."

On another occasion, she recalled that when she came to visit George, he was all upset. When she asked why, he told her that he had just organized his entire record collection, and the poltergeist and taken every record and placed them in precarious positions throughout the room. Although George doesn't remember this particular incident, he says that it probably did happen. There was just so much activity, that he stopped paying attention.

He does remember, however, this his next door neighbors also had a bad problem with ghosts. The neighbor's haunting seemed to be more severe than the Johnson's. On one occasion, before he knew about the haunting, George went across the street to their house and had a bone-chilling experience with a ghost. As George says, "The house across the street was definitely haunted. I didn't know it at the time. I was in the garage of the house across the street. It was the middle of the summer. It was hot as hell. And I walked into a little area of the garage and I got a cold chill. There was a cold spot in the garage. I asked the guy who was living there, and he said the previous owner had hung herself there."

Later on, George was to find out about a lot of other activity that had been occurring there. As he says, "All kinds of stuff used to happen in that house. They'd be gone, and we'd know they were gone and you'd look over and all the windows and doors would be open. And that happened several times. And all of the knives would disappear out of the house, all the fine cutlery, never come back, flat disappeared. That house had a lot of negative activity. Definitely."

When George reached eighteen years of age, he moved back to Kansas where he had relatives. He stayed there for a year, then returned back to California. He then joined the Navy, which was somewhat of a family tradition. Around the same time, his mom sold the house, which as far as George knew, was still haunted.

Since leaving the house and joining the Navy, George has had no poltergeist activity. However, for many years, he did have a ghost that followed him around. It first appeared right after he left the house and moved to Kansas. George surmised that it might be a sort of guardian angel or spirit guide. The ghost would often appear to him when he was going through tough times. It never really bothered him until one time when he saw it with his child. As George says, "He was a dark guy, really tall. A little dark, kind of shadowy dark, but not bad. Not a bad feeling. A real big guy. It was like a guardian angel. Because when I had different things going on in my life, it would appear."

Eventually, George married and had children. The ghost would make periodic appearances, but never in a threatening way. "I finally told it to go away because it bothered me. I saw it leaning over my kid's crib one time and it bothered me. So I told him to go and that was it. I haven't seen him since." George was in his mid-twenties when he told the ghost to leave.

Since then George has had no further ghost experiences, nor does he have any desire to try to contact ghosts or communicate with them. His case is typical of poltergeists. But what exactly caused the haunting is difficult to pinpoint. The haunting follows the pattern of being focused around a young child going through puberty. But explaining the activity as originating entirely from the repressed emotions of George doesn't really account for the wide range of activity. There was also the neighbor's haunting which may or may not have been related.

It is hard to say whether George's ghost was a deceased human, a poltergeist, a demon or the result of uncontrolled mediumship. George admits that he is somewhat psychic, but he certainly doesn't think of himself as a medium. Nevertheless, his experiences with the large dark guardian spirit strongly indicate that George does have some mediumistic capabilities.

George's reaction to the ghost was probably the correct one. Hauntings of this type can escalate to full-blown paranormal sieges, leading even to possession. By not reacting with fear and by not giving the ghost too much attention, the poltergeist was not getting what it wanted.

Perhaps for this reason, the poltergeist never went to the stage of possession. The fact that George continued to see a ghost for years after moving out of the house seems to support the theory that George does have some mediumistic talent. However, his decision to tell the ghost to leave and not come back did not cause an explosion of uncontrolled poltergeist activity.

Ultimately, whatever caused the poltergeist to come and go remains a mystery. All George knows is he experienced a poltergeist haunting firsthand. It is not a matter of belief; he knows that ghosts are real.

# 14 – A Brother's Ghost

One of the saddest of all of life's tragedies is the death of a child. When a young life is cut short, it is much different than the death of someone who has lived a long life. The death of children is hard to understand, and for many of the surviving family members, the grief can be overwhelming. Not only do the parents have trouble adjusting to the loss, but the deceased person's siblings can be just as deeply affected.

Tom Walker (pseudonym) of Los Angeles, California was living a normal life with his mother, father and brother. Then, in the early 1970s, Tom's life was drastically changed by the death of his older brother, Jeffrey (pseud-onym).

Jeffrey had a good job and was about to married when he was involved in a tragic car accident. He died at the scene of fatal injuries sustained in the accident.

Tom was devastated by his brother's death. He became very depressed and couldn't stop thinking about what had happened. He simply couldn't let go of the brother whom he had idolized and loved. For weeks afterwards, he remained gloomy, not wanting to live a life that suddenly seemed so empty. His parents tried to help, but they were so distraught by Jeffrey's death that there was little they could do other than offer their love. Tom's friends were also unable to lift him out of his dark depression.

Everyone knew Tom was depressed by his brother's death, but nobody realized how far his depression actually went. Tom never thought of commit-ting suicide. However, his love for his brother was so strong, that he found a way to transcend the barrier between life and death.

Before his death, Jeffrey had his own room. In his room he had a large swinging chair hanging from a hook in the ceiling. The chair was very heavy so he used metal chains to hang the chair. One of his favorite things to do was to sit in the chair and swing back and forth while listening to rock music. Tom would often find his brother spending his time in this way.

A few weeks after Jeffrey's death, Tom made a bizarre discovery. He had been mourning the loss of his brother, and for old time's sake, he had been playing some of the rock music his brother used to listen to while swinging in the chair. He turned the music on very loud, and just sat on the bed, imagin-ing and remembering what it was like when his brother was still alive.

Suddenly, to Tom's amazement, the hanging chair began to creak, and slowly move back and forth. In less than a minute, it was swinging back and forth in huge arcs, just as if somebody was sitting in it. Tom stared at the swing in awe. He knew instantly what was making the swing move, or rather who. It was his dead brother. There was no doubt in his mind whatsoever. He just knew that it his brother was sitting in the chair at that moment, listening to the music. He could literally feel Jeffrey's presence.

Eventually the swinging stopped. Tom, however, was transformed. His brother was still alive! He was a ghost, sure, but he was still around. Tom was delighted, and it wasn't long before he tried to call his brother's ghost again. Tom soon discovered that he could call his brother to the swing anytime he wanted. All he had to do was turn on the tape player to high volume, and play a certain song. The song was Pink Floyd's, *Comfortably Numb*. Every time Tom played this particular song, the swing would start to rock back and forth of its own accord, just as if somebody was sitting in it.

Tom couldn't believe what was happening and he finally decided to share his secret with someone. He chose his friend, Christine Dennett. One day, he invited Christine over and told her his secret, that he could call on the spirit of his dead brother for her, if she wanted him to do so. Christine was a little shocked, but saw no reason why not to try it. It sounded interesting and Tom certainly seemed sincere. Christine was sure he wasn't joking, but she couldn't believe her eyes when Tom turned on the music, and the chair began to move all by itself.

As Christine says, "He had a chair that hung from a chain that didn't touch the ground. It was like a swinging chair. And he said he could get his dead brother to sit in the chair and swing it when the music was on. And he'd turn on the music really loud, and the chair would swing.

"I saw it happen. He would just turn on the music and the chair would slowly start in a teeny little swing, and then get bigger and bigger and bigger. And then it would just swing, all by itself. Nobody was there making it swing.

"It was a heavy chair, but it was taut as if somebody was sitting in it. It wasn't floating in any way."

Christine tried to figure out how the event could have been faked, but it seemed impossible. The chair was behaving exactly as if somebody was swinging in it. Tom seemed very casual about the whole affair, and seemed comfortable with the knowledge that his brother's spirit was still around.

The incident convinced Christine even more that ghosts were real. For Tom, however, it made all the difference in the world. He slowly lifted out of his depression and began to lead a normal life. He eventually stopped calling his brother's spirit, as there was simply no need to do so. He was satisfied that life continues after death, and that one day, he would see his brother again. It is just one more case of how love can transcend all barriers, including death.

# 15 – The Haunted Armoire

Christine Dennett is no stranger to ghosts. Not only did two of her best friends have regular encounters with ghosts, she herself lived in a haunted house. The house is located in Woodland Hills, California, and was new when Christine moved in with her sister and parents. As they grew up, both sisters felt that there was a ghost in the house, though nothing actually ever happened.

Then many, many years later, Christine had married and was sleeping the house with her husband. She woke up one night to witness incontrovertible and physical proof that ghosts are real. As she says, "I lived all my life in Woodland Hills and I lived in a house where I believed there were spirits. One particular night, my mother left and asked me and my husband to house-sit. So we were sleeping in her bed. And I have a sensitivity about that house. I always wake up at witching hour, at three-thirty about, and I'll stay up for about an hour. Well this particular night I just woke up out of a dead sleep, wide awake, and sat up in bed. My husband was beside me sound asleep.

"And I looked up and I saw in front of me an armoire, which is a portable closet. It is a big, huge, gigantic piece of furniture. And on the door was a latch. This particular latch, you have to turn it to the side, to the right, upwards. It's a hanging latch, a pretty little, brass, oval-shaped latch. And you touch the latch and you push it up to the side, and it opens the door.

"Well, as I was up that night looking at the armoire, my eyes automatically went to the armoire. I saw the latch lift up all by itself, and slightly open the door. The door opened about four inches. As I was watching this happen, I know my husband has never experienced a ghost. So I wanted him to see this. So I turned over. He was on my right side. And I was shaking him. I said, 'Wake up! Wake up!' And I tried to wake him up so hard. And I was trying to be quiet so I wouldn't scare the ghost away either. And he would not wake up. No way. I was shaking him hard too. And I looked up, and I saw the latch lift up again, and the door slowly close shut. And I'm thinking, 'Oh, dammit! He didn't wake up. He missed his chance to see a ghost.'"

On another occasion, Christine and her husband were again house sitting, this time sleeping in her bed. It was to be another strange, haunting night. Her husband was unable to sleep in the bed and eventually left. Christine also had trouble sleeping, and soon found out what was bothering them. It was a ghost. As she says, "He eventually got out of bed and slept somewhere else. And I stayed in the bed and every once in a while, right when I was just ready to go to sleep, the bed would shake. It would shake and wake me up. I didn't sleep that whole night. Because every time I would almost get to sleep, the bed would start shaking."

Both of Christine's children have experienced ghostly activity. Her daughter has seen outlines of apparitions on a few occasions. Her son has also experienced activity. As her son says, "I was in the room in-between our house and grandma's house. And I closed the windows and I locked them. And I walked out to talk to you and you were in Grandma's kitchen with Grandma. And you and I were the only ones there. And I walked over to talk to you and when I came back in, the door was open, and the windows were open, and nobody else was there."

On another night, her son, then nine-years-old, decided to spend the night alone. This was soon after Christine's experience with the bed-shaking. Her son tried to fall asleep, but the ghosts became suddenly active. As he says, "I just couldn't get to sleep because I heard noises. I heard like people talking, more than one. In the house I heard people talking and walking around, outside my room."

At first he just shrugged off the activity. Then something happened which made him want to leave immediately. As he says, "I closed all the cabinets in the kitchen when I left to get Zabba [the dog] out from the bedroom. And I came back and all the cabinets were open again."

He also reports strange activity around the armoire. As he says, "There were all these blurry marks flying around the dresser, the big dresser. All these blurry spots were flying around it. I saw like three or four blurry spots like coming out from the back and flying down and forwards and criss-crossing."

Christine's sister, Cathy, also grew up in the house. She is a firm believer that the house is haunted. As she says, "All my life I experienced strange occurrences in that house."

Most often, it was just the feeling of a presence which became so strong, it would make Cathy turn around.

She wouldn't see anybody, but she could sense that somebody was there. She would shout at them to go away.

Sometimes, however, the activity became stronger. Says Cathy, "When I was growing up in that house, there was one night when everybody was gone and I was alone. I think I was about sixteen years old [1977]. And all night long, the doors were shutting. It just wasn't a comfortable evening. I kept saying, 'Leave me alone! Whoever you are, leave me alone!'

"And there were weird things cracking, noises that weren't normally there were happening in the house. And I felt like I was having this little battle with something. It was a very interesting evening. I didn't like it, but I stayed there. I stayed home. Sometimes I would leave when it would get like that. I didn't like it. I would leave."

Cathy had no idea what was causing the activity, but for some reason, she thought it had something to do with the armoire. She didn't yet know about Christine's experiences.

Cathy's next encounter involved being woken up by the ghost. "I was asleep. I woke up out of my sleep and really felt like something was standing over me. I just sensed it. So I said, 'Here we go again.' So I went through this whole thing of, 'Please, leave! I don't want to be disturbed. Leave me alone!' And I could sort of feel, sense something leaving. And then I was hearing noises in the armoire. It just sort of cracked and creaked, and I just kind of had a feeling that it had to do with that armoire. And then Christy told me stories about it opening and stuff. So then it made more sense to me. So for me it was just a sensation. It was more a feeling. It's almost like if you closed your eyes, you would think someone was standing there. But they wouldn't be there when your eyes opened. Ever get the feeling of somebody walking into the room and you know it? It was the same sensation."

Christine never did figure out why that particular armoire was haunted, or if it was the cause of the other activity in the house. A professional medium once did a walk through the house. As Christine says, "He sat down in the house, and he closed his eyes, and he went into a trance state. And he saw this woman with black hair down to her waist, past her waist, wearing this long robe. And she was holding this huge Bible. And she had a big, huge gold cross on her chest. And she just walked, strolled across the living room."

Christine's mother, who just recently sold the house, has never reported any ghostly activity whatsoever. There was one time, however, when she bought another antique armoire. She had to get rid of it because both Christine and her sister had horrible nightmares that a little girl had died in the armoire.

Christine reports that she often felt the presence of someone in the house, though other than the above activity, the ghost never really manifested. She remembers a humorous incident where their cat disappeared inside one closet to come out on the opposite wall as if it had walked through the wall. Otherwise, the house is very much a typical suburban home.

Like many other homes, there just may be a spirit that resides peacefully along with the living residents. Stranger things have happened.

# 16 – The Ghost Dog

Topanga Canyon is the location of several of the accounts in this book. Located just outside the sprawling metropolis of Los Angeles, it still remains an outpost of wilderness, complete with cougars, bobcats, fox, coyote, raccoon, owls, rabbits, deer and more. The road through the canyon is long and winding. There are no street lights or sidewalks, and only one stoplight. Parts of the road are fairly isolated from houses and other buildings.

Late one night in November, 1994, longtime Topanga resident, Mimi Smith was driving through the canyon when she encountered one of the strangest things she has ever seen. At first she thought it was an animal crossing the road. However, not only did it look strange, it moved strangely. But it wasn't until it turned and looked at her that Mimi got the shock of her life. It was standing right in front of her headlights, staring at her with eye-holes that were completely empty! As Mimi says, "I'm coming home between eleven thirty and twelve midnight, and as I pulled down the grade going into the canyon, I saw what appeared to be an animal in the street. I slammed on the brakes and pulled over to the side. It appeared to be like a sheep. Let me tell you, it was very strange. It was on one side of the road, and it was standing there. It was shaped like a sheep, and its head was round and placed lower on its body, and it appeared almost as if it had waggled on some kind of spring.

"So I waited and it crossed the road. And it didn't go with footsteps. It moved like it glided along. As I looked at it, I saw that its eyes in its head were like holes, with nothing there. You could see through. If you looked at the thing's eyes, you could the fence posts in back of it. In other words, it was like they were hollow. There weren't any eyes. It had round holes. And it had a little mouth, you know how some dogs have brownish lips. And then it just kept right on going. It went down the other side of the mountain. And it was one of the strangest things I have ever seen up here. We've been up here for thirty-seven years, and we've ridden the mountains a lot and seen a lot of things."

Mimi was stunned by how strange the creature looked. She knows it was not a normal creature. As she says, "When I put on the brakes, I thought somebody's sheep had gotten out, that was my very first thought. It was dirty-white, all funky dirty, made out of like dirty cotton. It looked like a real dirty sheep. The hair was – it wasn't hair like we're thinking of hair. Think of a thing made of a closely densely packed fog. And then the eyes, it looked right at me, walked across and just looked right at me. My first thought, as I say, I thought it was a live animal. I slammed on the brakes. And then I saw that it wasn't and I wasn't about to do anything. I was just transfixed with looking at it. And as it crossed to go down on the other side, I looked right at its eyes, and you could see the fenceposts behind its eyes, like you're looking through. I wasn't afraid. I wasn't terrified. I didn't feel like I was going to be attacked. I felt, if anything, this thing is going to take its time and I wish I wasn't here. I mean, a feeling like I don't want to mess with it. I mean, I see this is something; we're not talking dog or sheep in the road."

Mimi is sure that what she saw was no normal creature. It was a mere ten feet in front of her headlights. There was no way that she could have misperceived it. And when she saw the fence posts through the eyeholes, she knew for sure that it was something supernatural. She later asked a Chumash Indian elder what he thought it was. As she says, "We consulted a friend of ours who is a Chumash medicine man. And his thoughts on the matter were that since it seemed to be going across the road from the left side to the right and down; and they've been doing some excavating up there on Santa Maria road, and there's all those Indian caves there – he just thought it was some kind of a spirit, because of all the earth-moving."

Mimi doesn't know for sure what she saw, but she leans towards the ghost dog explanation. As she says, "I realized with a shock that you could see the places where its eyes were. I realized you could look right through its eyes. I don't know. I just think it was some kind of very bizarre spirit. I know they abound in the canyon. I know other people have seen lots of other strange things like that."

Could Mimi have just been perceiving a normal creature? This is doubtful. She insists that she has seen the myriad of wildlife that lives in Topanga, and that what she saw was not anything that normally lives out in the wild. The fact that she could see right through the eye-holes confirmed to her that it was not really a creature at all, but a ghost. She had no idea that many other people have described similar accounts of ghosts with no eyes.

Mimi reports that she actually saw the ghost dog on another occasion a few months later. On both occasions, the same thing happened; it crossed the road, she stopped and as it looked at her, she saw right through the eye holes. The second incident happened at nearly the exact same location along the road. Again, Mimi was certain that she was not misperceiving. The way the creature seemed to float, its almost foggy appearance, its strange shape, and hollow eyes all point to the fact that she saw something that was definitely not a normal dog.

Since then, she has not had any further encounters with the ghost dog of Topanga.

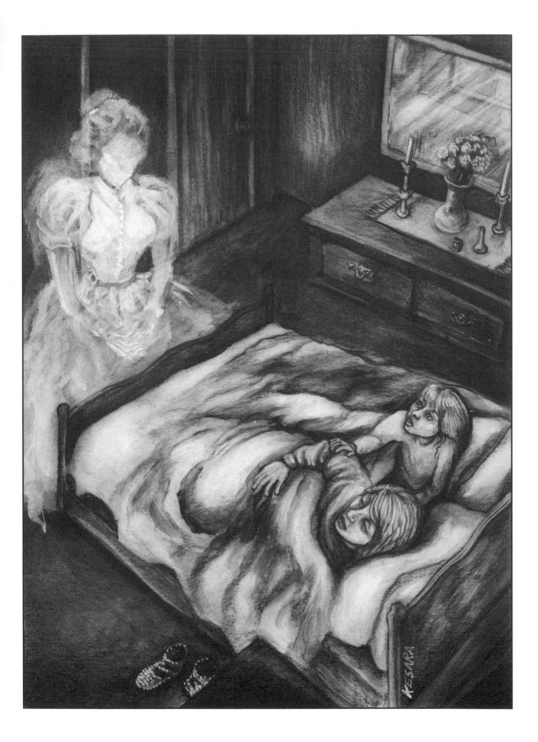

# 17 – The Coldness of Ghosts

Ardelle Kelly Levy was only eight years old when she saw her first ghost. Kelly (as she prefers to be called) was born into a family full of mediums. Her mother saw ghosts. So did her grandmother. And her aunt. Even Kelly's children have reported their own encounters. Evidently, the ability to see ghosts can run in families.

Her first experience occurred in her home in the Midwest. She was sleeping in the same room with her grandmother when she woke up to see an incredible sight. "I was frightened to look. I couldn't understand it because I had gone to sleep and there were just the two of us in the room. I remember feeling a coldness, then I looked up at the end of the bed and there was this figure. This white figure, female…but I remember my grandmother was talking and gesturing and moving her arms…the apparition, I could see a female in an old-fashioned dress."

Kelly was amazed to see that her grandmother was actually carrying on a conversation with the ghost. Says Kelly, "They were talking. I reached over and grabbed my grandmother. I said, 'Grandma! Grandma!' And she said, 'Just a minute!'

"I was absolutely terrified. And the minute I introduced myself into this dialogue, this conversation, my grandmother said something like, 'Okay, we'll discuss this later.' In other words, she was dismissing the apparition and the apparition was disappearing. I said, 'Grandma, that was a ghost! You were talking to a ghost!'

"And my grandmother said, 'Well, yes, but that was my sister. We talk a lot. Don't be afraid. There's nothing wrong with seeing ghosts."

Kelly's early experience with the supernatural gave her the education she would need to support her through her many future experiences. She never had a problem believing in ghosts simply because she never had a chance! Her grandmother revealed that most of the women in their family saw ghosts, and that it was something she better get used to.

Following this experience, Kelly had no further experiences with ghosts. At least not at first. She grew up, became engaged, and moved to Sylmar, California with her husband.

The year was 1960. Kelly had almost completely forgotten about her childhood ghost encounter. She was busy trying to settle in her new life with her future husband. They were staying temporarily in her fiancée's parents' house.

Kelly had a job interview the next morning, so she went to bed alone early. Says Kelly, "I went into this bedroom and I felt very uncomfortable. I didn't know why at this point, but just horribly uncomfortable. I remember going to the door and calling [my fiancée's] name, calling it very faintly. And he didn't come. I just decided, 'Oh, heck with it, I might as well relax and try to go to sleep. I went back to bed. There were two windows in this bedroom. I was in the twin bed and the head was at the window. And the other window was alongside of the bed. And as I got into the bed, all of a sudden I was extremely cold. I was just freezing. Now this is July and we're in the San Fernando Valley in Sylmar. It's not cold, right? And I was extremely cold. And I thought, 'Oh, this is ridiculous!'

"I pulled the covers up and then I sat up. I thought, 'Oh, my God, there's something here! There's somebody here. There's somebody watching me.'

"My first thought was, 'My God, what are you doing?' But I knew that there was something really amiss. There was something wrong here. And I turned around and I looked out the window that was right at the head of the bed. And there was a figure. And it appeared as though it was outside, or right on top of the window. I couldn't tell whether it was male or female. For some reason I thought it was a male figure. And my first inclination, of course, was that there was a Peeping Tom.

"It seemed as though it had a plaid shirt on. It was like a darker blue-gray and then lighter in shades of white and blue. He was just standing there. There was no talking or gesturing or anything. But there was a short-sleeved plaid shirt and a very short haircut. I don't remember him being an especially large person, but I knew it was a man. It looked solid, but the interesting thing was, I was seeing it as clearly through the window-shade as I was through the screen. It must have been right on the window-shade. I could see his face. Maybe that's why I can remember the eyes because it was definitely looking at me. It never moved. It was just totally still. The arms were at his side. The mouth never moved. But the eyes were looking at me.

"And I'm looking at this. And I turned and put my head under the covers. But nothing happened. It was really cold. I remember sitting on the side of the bed, looking at this, saying, 'Go away! Go away!' And this apparition just stayed in place. Well then I put my feet and head back in bed and covered up my whole self, my head. You think about the stupid things you do. If that had been a real person, a lot of good that would have done. But at the time, I was just absolutely terrified.

"And all of a sudden the coldness just went away. I glanced over to the side. There had been this light emanating from the side, obviously from the apparition. And it was gone. The room was totally dark. At that point I didn't know what to do."

Kelly decided to go to sleep. The next morning she rushed off to her interview. She didn't tell anyone about her experience and filed it in the back of her mind. Her life was going through so much change at the time, she didn't want to add the burden of an unexplained ghostly encounter.

However, a few months later, she returned to the house to celebrate the Thanksgiving holiday. She was at the home, having a good time when she walked by the bedroom where she had seen the ghost. She suddenly became unaccountably terrified. She instantly realized that the source of her fear was the bedroom where she had her encounter. It got so bad that she finally mentioned it to her husband. It was then that she discovered the reason for her feelings.

Her husband said that the house was haunted and had been ever since he was a child. The previous owners had a seventeen-year-old child who was killed in a motorcycle accident. The grieving parents sold the house after many strange incidents began to happen.

Soon after the new family (Kelly's in-laws) moved in, they noticed odd activity. Kelly's husband says, "I do remember that sometimes where would be a real coldness and I knew there was somebody watching me."

The activity became so unnerving that the family sat down one evening and demanded, out loud, that the ghost leave. Remarkably, that seemed to stop the activity. Although they sometimes still felt the strange presence, there had been no disturbing incidents for years. It wasn't until Kelly confessed her recent encounter that they realized the ghost was still around.

At first, Kelly assumed it was an amazing coincidence that she had seen ghosts twice. However, she was soon to discover that ghosts are much more common than most people realize, and that many people lived in haunted houses.

In 1970, she and her family went to visit a relative's home in Beverly Hills, California. It was a very old two-story house. Kelly had been there before and had never experienced anything strange. However, her cousin was keeping a secret about the house. Unknown to Kelly, it was badly haunted. Her cousin had kept silent for obvious reasons.

Therefore Kelly had no warning whatsoever that she was about to walk into the most horrifying experience of her life. Says Kelly, "I had been there before. I had been there after. But I don't think I ever went upstairs after this happened. Anyway, as you walked into the house, there was an entryway and the stairway was immediately in front of you. You would walk upstairs and on the upper corridor of the hall there was the bathroom. The door to the bathroom was almost directly in line with the stairway as you entered. And there was a bedroom to the right and two bedrooms down the hall to the left.

"The children were downstairs. My husband was downstairs. Everybody was downstairs. I went upstairs and went to the bathroom. And as I came out of the bathroom and headed towards the stairway which was maybe six feet in front of me, I was pushed very, very hard from behind. I remember stumbling, and I turned around and there was no one there. And I stood up. I almost lost my balance. I looked and I said, 'What on Earth?'

"And with that I was pushed. I mean, I was facing where I had been standing, and all of a sudden I was pushed on my arm, and I was literally pushed into this bedroom. The door was open. And what I did was – I remember going past the door and thinking, 'Oh, my God! I can't let this door be shut!' At that time, I whirled and grabbed onto the door handle. And once again, there was this very, very cold feeling. At first I thought, 'Oh, my God! Maybe I'm getting sick! Maybe I'm starting to faint!' I was in a cold sweat.

"There was nothing ever said. I never saw an apparition. I had no idea what on Earth this thing was. But as quickly as this wave of coldness swept over me, it was gone. I remember grabbing hold of the door and holding on really tight. The door was open, but I was afraid somehow that I was going to get shut in there. I didn't know. So I grabbed a hold of the door and I remember getting control of myself and regaining my composure and walking downstairs. I didn't say anything until we got home."

Kelly reports that whoever or whatever the ghost was, it was very strong. It felt exactly as if unseen hands were pushing her around. As she says, "It was like a hand in the middle of the back. And then when I turned around to see this, I was pushed a second time and it was also like a hand, but I couldn't see anything."

Two weeks later, she visited her cousin and decided to reveal her experience. To her surprise, they apologized and said that they were already aware of the ghost and had many problems with it. In fact, they had called the UCLA parapsychology department who sent over psychics and researchers. Their investigation revealed that the house was haunted by two ghosts. One was reportedly benevolent and was a member of the family that had been killed. This ghost was apparently there to protect the family from the other ghost, which was not benevolent.

Kelly's cousin reported that she too had been pushed by the ghost and nearly thrown down the stairs. Her daughter had also been physically assaulted by the ghost and had seen apparitions on several occasions. Each time she would feel a strong drop in temperature, and then would turn around and see the apparition of an older man staring at her. Many others in the house had been touched, poked, slapped or pushed by the ghost. The crew from UCLA eventually organized a formal exorcism, but it didn't work. The family finally moved out of the house because they couldn't handle any more of the ghost activity.

Kelly continues to have experiences with ghosts. What most impresses her about these visitations is the coldness. As she says, "The thing that I remember was the coldness. In retrospect, I realize that along with these experiences there seems to be an element of cold air that accompanies them."

Kelly was surprised to learn that this coldness is actually a common feature of ghosts, particularly when there is a physical manifestation. Some researchers have theorized that ghosts are actually able to utilize the heat energy of the room in order to materialize. Whatever the case, the coldness of ghosts is something Kelly has felt many times. And with her track record, it is likely that she will feel it again.

# 18 – A Hand Across Death

While many ghosts are people who aren't aware that they have died, this is not always the case. Some ghosts know perfectly well that they have died. These types of ghosts usually appear because they have a purpose, some unfinished business to resolve. This could be anything from revealing a hidden will to exposing the guilt of one's murderer. The possibilities are endless. In the following case, it was unrequited love that caused a ghost to return from the other side. While most ghosts manifest in the form of apparitions, smells or unexplained sounds, this ghost was able to leave physical evidence of its presence.

Connie Lopez (now in her mid-fifties) is the mother of three full grown children. She works full time and lives alone in her West Hills, California townhome. She had never seen a ghost in her entire life. But all that changed in September 2001.

Says Connie, "This is what happened. I got up as regular, the everyday normal thing – to go and get ready for work. The first thing I did was to go into the shower. And when I opened the door, I saw a handprint, an oil handprint on the tile. And I was in shock because of the fact that I don't like anything dirty or greasy in the house. And to see that handprint on the tile, it just got me really scared because I thought somebody was in the house….it was really strange. I put my finger on it and I smelled it. And it was oil. It was a handprint. What I even did was put my hand close to it to see if it was a bigger hand or a smaller hand. It was bigger than mine…I mean I really got really scared.

"[It was] regular car oil. I even touched it with one of my fingers real lightly and I smelled it. I thought, car oil? Who would be in my house with car oil? Because I have everything clean. I'm really spotless. So I was really surprised. I was *really, really* surprised. I thought, who in the heck? But then I just got really scared, and I scrubbed it off."

Connie checked the house to make sure all the windows and doors were locked. She called the manager and asked if anybody had entered her home for repairs. She checked the bathroom thoroughly for any possible source of the oil. Nothing could explain it. Says Connie, "It really scared me because I kept thinking, God, I wonder if somebody's finding a way to come into my house?"

Connie tried not to think about what had happened. She already had enough problems to think about. Six months earlier, her ex-husband, Mario (not his real name) whom she hadn't seen in twenty years had called her up out of the blue. He needed a place to live. He worked as a trucker, and really only needed a small place to store his things. Most of the time he would be out on the road.

Connie found herself agreeing to rent him a room in her home. Her only condition was that he keep the house clean. Because he was a trucker, he was often up to his elbows in his engine, fixing and repairing it. Connie always made him leave his oily boots outside on the doorstep. Mario happily obliged.

Otherwise, they lived together in harmony, platonically. Mario, however, never wavered in his love for Connie. In all the years following the divorce, he called her on every birthday, Christmas and major holiday. Although Connie assured him that their relationship was over, Mario professed his undying love for her.

Despite the awkwardness of their living situation, things were going great. Then tragedy struck. Mario went out to a party and never came home. Connie learned that he suffered a major heart attack and died on the scene. He was forty-nine years old.

Connie was devastated and heart-broken. She learned that Mario actually knew he had a weak heart and was likely to perish soon. And yet he chose to live the last months of his life with her. And now he was dead.

So Connie was already upset and grieving when she now had the added problem of a possible intruder in her home. She couldn't explain the oily handprint. It just didn't make any sense. So she cleaned it up and tried not to think about it.

Then a few days later, the unknown intruder returned. Connie explains, "I woke up. I sat up, and I fixed my bed like normal. I started walking down the hall and I turned the light on. And the bathroom's really nice and bright because of the window. I put my hand on the handle to open the shower, and I saw this handprint right *on* my hand. I mean, there was an oil handprint on top of my hand, like somebody had grabbed my hand and left their handprint right on top of my hand. Like somebody had just put their hand on my hand when I was asleep or something. It left a handprint right on my hand!

"When I looked at it, I said, 'Oh, my God! What!' And I touched it with my finger again. It was oil. I smelled oil. It was car oil, but on my hand! But that was not even it. What happened was, I got scared. I walked into my room. I looked around my room. I pulled the sheets up to see if there was any oil on the bed, anywhere. I turned on the lights. I opened the blinds. And guess what? There were oil spots around my bed. As a matter of fact, the oil spots are still around the bed, like somebody went around the bed dropping oil."

Connie was shocked. She hurriedly wiped the oil off her hand and cleaned up the mess around her bed. She again checked all the doors and windows. She examined the ceiling and walls around her bed, looking for a solution to the mystery. Says Connie, "I was in shock. I was totally in shock. But then what I realized is when I came downstairs in my dining area, someone went around my dining area with oil! They did the same thing around my dining area, like they purposely went around the table, like somebody was just splattering it. Not like little drops here and there, but like somebody got a can of oil and was just making lines back and forth, streaks and lines of oil. I said, something's wrong here. Who would come in my house and just splatter oil all over my carpet and only around the dining area, which was so strange because it stayed mostly on the corner. I couldn't believe it. I had bar stools, and it was right around the bar stools, like somebody just sat there, splattering it. I was just so puzzled about it, I could not even believe it."

Connie again assumed that somebody must have come into the house. She called up the manager and accused him of having given away her keys. He denied it. She asked him again if they had come into her house with oil to make repairs. Again, he replied in the negative.

Connie then revealed her problem. The manager was as mystified as she was. He assured her that it wasn't the building or him. The carpet itself was new. There seemed to be no explanation.

Then, as Connie began the difficult task of cleaning up the oil in the dining room, she had a sudden revelation. She remembered having had to clean up oil stains on her carpet before. Over and over again, Mario would come into the house with his oily hands, boots, and clothes and leave oil stains on the couch, floor, counters, wherever he touched. It infuriated her and he *knew* it.

Connie felt chills race down her spine. Suddenly all the pieces began to fall into place: Mario's obsessive love for her, his profession as a truck driver and mechanic that left him oily, Connie's obsessive need for cleanliness, Mario's death, her devastation at his death, and now this. Oil all over her house. And the large handprint on her shower, and then the handprint grasping her hand. The answer was so obvious, she was surprised she hadn't hit upon it sooner. It was Mario. Mario's ghost was trying to get in contact with her, trying to communicate to her that he was all right.

Says Connie, "He was a truck driver. He was always messing around with oil. *Always*. Fixing his car, cleaning his truck. And I always used to tell him, 'You need to take off your boots outside. Do not come in the house with your boots because they're full of oil.' That's when it dawned on me. I kept thinking to myself, 'Oh, my God!' I was so scared. But it really honestly happened. It happened to me twice. And I can't believe when I was looking for the oil, why would somebody put oil around my bed? And to put oil around my dining area!"

Now Connie believes that Mario came back and as a kind of personal joke, left oily handprints and stains around her house one last time. As Connie says, "Can you believe that? Like he's saying, 'Now, I'm gone. Now, what are you going to do?' You know what I mean? You can't say anything anymore. And here are the oil stains. Oh, my God, I was so scared. At first I was really shocked. But after that, everyone kept telling me he really cared about you, that's why he probably tried to come back. But to throw oil, to tell me, 'Now what are you going to do?' But he let me know he's been here, that he's been in my house. Believe me, I have the oil stains still in my bedroom."

Connie told Mario's family what happened, and to her shock, they told her that Mario had also appeared to them. His daughter and the neighbor's three-year-old little girl each claimed to have seen his apparition. They all believed Connie, and were amazed at how Mario manifested his presence to her; using car oil was the perfect way to let her know that it was really him.

While Connie now receives a measure of comfort from her experience, it still causes her some fear. The carpet is now permanently stained as a reminder of her experience. She even rearranged her furniture to cover the stains because, as she says, "Every time I see it, it's really scary. I hope I never have to experience something like that again."

# 19 – Adventures in Table Lifting

In 1955, Margaret Johnson (pseudonym) went to attend college along the eastern coast of the United States. She joined a sorority and prepared for her new life. When she arrived, she got an incredible shock. Her sorority sisters somehow knew everything about her life. They named her family, how many brothers and sisters she had, what she had chosen for her major, the name of her boyfriend, and numerous other personal details that were beyond their ability to know. Amazed, Margaret asked them how they did it.

The girls giggled and let her in on their secret. They used a method called table lifting (also called table tipping or table rapping). Essentially a variation of the Ouija board, two or more people sit around a table and place their hands lightly on the surface. After saying a prayer, they ask for the spirits to come and lift the table. If conditions are correct, the table will rise on two legs, or even completely levitate. Questions can then be asked of various spirits.

The girls proceeded to give Margaret a demonstration and proved to her instantly that table lifting was a true phenomenon. As it turned out, Margaret herself was particularly talented at it, and after learning from her roommates, became very proficient. They held numerous séances and were able to produce a number of physical effects. Margaret claims that not only would the table levitate completely off the floor, but candle flames could be made to grow brighter or become extinguished, and sometimes various objects would move, such as pictures flying off the walls.

After college, Margaret moved to Woodland Hills, California where she raised a family. In 1989, she worked at a shirt company, painting designs on clothes.

At the same company was another lady, Deborah Carlson (pseudonym) who also painted shirts, and the two of them became friends.

One day Margaret told Deborah about her secret talent of table lifting and took her to a session. To Deborah's astonishment, Margaret set her hand lightly on a small card table, and it began to dance underneath her fingertips.

Says Deborah, "It was just a small metal table. Once Margaret brought the table and had it rapping, she asked the table questions. And she asked about a former teacher of hers that was murdered. And it told the date that this person was murdered, and it said that they still did not know who the killer was. And then we ended it."

Although the session was short, Deborah was very impressed. As she says, "I was there. I was a witness, and I thought, 'I still don't understand it. Why did it do that?' And these were believable people. What would they have to gain from flaunting it?"

In fact, Deborah was so impressed, she wanted to try it herself. She had no idea if she could do it, but it seemed easy enough. And it couldn't hurt to try. She decided to ask her teen-age kids if they would like to try it. Little did she know that this single decision would cause a huge shift in her life.

Says Deborah, "About a week later, I told the kids what I had seen because I couldn't believe it. So I asked the kids if they would like to try it. And we tried it. And I don't know, it just sort of moved slightly. Then we tried it again about a week later, and the table actually came up on two legs. It twisted. It moved approximately five feet. That second time that we finally got it up, I said, 'Is this my mother? If it is, rap twice.' And it did. And I said, 'Are you glad that we brought you to the table to communicate with us?' And that's when it really rocked. It was just a happy medium."

Deborah and her kids talked with her deceased mother for several minutes. Then Deborah's husband, Daniel, came home. Deborah asked him if he wanted to talk to his deceased father, but he was skeptical about what was happening and refused. At that point, the table began to rock strangely. Says Deborah, "The table just sort of twisted back and forth like there was a turmoil going on inside – a feud. When there are two spirits fighting to communicate, a lot of times you can just feel the tension in the table, the way it's rocking, in its movement. You could tell it was there. And Daniel walked away. He said, 'I can't talk to my father.' And the minute he said that, the table stopped. There was just no more to it."

Deborah, however, was persistent. She laid her hands back on the table with her children, and they called again for her mother. The table rose on two legs instantly. Says Deborah, "That's when it moved the five feet. We had to get up and move out of our chairs to keep up with it. It was like it scooted. The only way I can describe it is it danced. Just across the room, back and forth, in just real happy movements. You know, it was bouncy. It sounds weird to talk about it, but that's the way it was. It was just rocking back and forth. I don't know, it was like it danced. That's the only way I can describe it. And I had such a warm feeling. We all started crying. We said, 'Mother, we have to go now. We love you." And it was just like she was there embracing us. I don't know how to explain it. There was no fear then. Even though I still couldn't explain how I did it, and I still can't to this day.

"We kept this up for about an hour. When the children and I did it, it actually worked. It was frightening, and yet, it wasn't. Because the person we seemed to be communicating with was my mother, who had just passed away in September."

After they finished, Deborah and her two children looked at each other in amazement. As she says, "Nobody wanted to stop. Once we did it, we were sort of in awe. And it was sort of frightening. You're afraid. You don't know how to explain this. But it's just a very enlightening feeling, with the kids, and they shared it too. Even though we all had this wide-eyed look, 'What have we done? What have we gotten ourselves into?' But it didn't really matter because we never felt threatened. It was just a nice feeling. The only way I can describe it is like she was there and she had her arms around all of us. There was just that love there. You could tell there was love and warmth."

After the session with her children, Deborah stopped for awhile. Instead, she read up on the subject to make sure that she knew exactly what she was doing. To her dismay, there was almost no information on table lifting. She learned that it was a popular parlor game before radio and television, especially in Europe. She learned that it is safe as long as proper precautions are taken, including saying a prayer before and after each session. She talked more with Margaret and learned that both she and her mother had been doing it for years.

Deborah decided she would try again. She practiced using a light wooden card table with four legs. Placing her fingers lightly on the table, she found that she was, in fact, able to make the table rise up on two legs.

It didn't work every time, but with practice she learned to regularly bring in various spirits and communicate with them.

Says Deborah, "Sometimes I can put my hand there [on the table] and it will immediately rock. And other times, it takes a few times. You can almost feel the coldness too when another person comes in. I just talk to my relatives. My mother's is like a lighter and happier type thing. And my grandmother, I don't know whether I just feel this or whether it's actually doing it because my grandmother's more impatient, she wants to just get along with it. And my grandfather is understanding, and his is a slow rocking. And my father's is a slow and gentle rocking and he doesn't stay very long. My mother is the one that just seems to hold on for the longest. And my grandmother comes through all the time. My other grandmother comes through…yeah, you can just tell. There's just a change, a slight change. It might just sort of twist a little bit and that's it. Or it might stop, and it just starts rocking again. And you'll go through this. It changes."

Deborah admits that she hasn't received much evidential information. But she does hear personal details and receives encouragement in dealing with other issues.

She normally says a prayer before and after each session. She learned the hard way how important this can be. As she says, "In reading books, what little I can find, it always says to say a prayer before you do it. One time, I didn't do that. And you could almost feel the animosity. It wasn't a good feeling at all. So we just stopped. I knew it wasn't my mother. And the table pounded. It didn't rock. When I'm communicating with a relative, it rocks gently. Even when it's excited, it's still a nice, gently, happy rock. And if you get someone in there you don't know who you're really talking to yet, it pounds. You can just tell – the anger in there or an animosity of some kind that's unexplainable."

What does Deborah do when things get out of control? Her solution is simple. "You just take your hands away from the table and it will stop."

What makes table lifting so unique and powerful is that it is essentially a *controlled haunting*. While ghostly manifestations usually occur at random, this method allows for ghosts to be brought into the laboratory for study. It is, in effect, easy access to the paranormal.

However, things can get out of control. Following the occasion where Deborah forgot to say a prayer, she experienced the feeling of an unpleasant presence roaming through her home. As she says, "There was something that was just not right. For like a week or so, it just felt like – I don't know. It just wasn't the same. A couple of times I have felt that I'm not alone, that someone's in the room with me. You can just tell, I don't know. But when you look, there's nothing really there…But there was a lot of times that there is a strong sensation that someone is there. But when you look and you check, you don't see anything."

A few other strange events occurred. Deborah was out by the community pool when she heard a strange clicking noise. It suddenly got very loud and moved right past her, and yet nothing was there. The incident scared her, and she had the feeling it was related to the table lifting.

Then there was an unexplained fire in the kitchen. Nobody was in the kitchen at the time. Deborah walked in and found a dish-rag on fire, on the stove. She has no idea how it happened or what it means. "I don't know whether that was something telling me – I don't know."

At that point, she considered calling the UCLA parapsychology department but instead decided to perform her own informal exorcism. As she says, "I finally just went through the house and just said, 'Get out! We don't need you here! I don't want you here! You don't belong here!' I started in with the thing, the prayers, and asking help from the good spirits telling them to get rid of it."

To her delight, the informal exorcism was completely successful. She suffered no further unpleasant incidents, and continued to perform table lifting sessions. She was eventually holding monthly sessions in her home for her friends and co-workers.

Around this time, a mother and artist named Christine Dennett (the illustrator for this book) applied for and received employment at the same company where Margaret and Deborah worked.

Christy was stunned to learn that her co-workers were holding séances. Due to several personal experiences, Christy already had a deep interest in the paranormal. To her delight, Margaret invited her over for a session.

Christy was amazed. It was a party-like atmosphere as the half-dozen women sat around a small table and began the séance. Christy was most impressed by the feeling of energy in the room. As she says, "I got this rushing feeling, like excitement. And then I felt my chair starting to wiggle underneath me. It was shaking a little bit, just a tiny little bit. And then I felt the shaking going up my body, into my arms and onto the table. And then the table started shaking. And it gave me the strange feeling that I was being used, that my body was transmitting something through it. So the table started rocking more and more and it was a very strong rocking."

Like Deborah, Christy also noticed that different spirits caused the table to move differently. As she says, "The table would hit the ground on one side. It would rock up so it was leaning on two legs, then it would down on the other two legs. Sometimes it would twist up and go up on three legs and be leaning on one leg.

"So then other spirits started coming through, and each time that other spirits came through, it felt different. The suicides were very strong. And the long deaths, the ones that took a long time to die – like one little girl that came through who passed away from cancer – she was very delicate. The table would move just a little bit, and it was very sweet and delicate. You could feel the energy because it would travel through you."

Following her experience, Christy called me up and asked me if I wanted to attend a session. Of course, I said yes. Little did I know, I was about to have one of the most amazing experiences of my life.

It was April 1989 and Christy and I drove to Deborah's house in Woodland Hills. It was a beautiful home, very expensive, and nicely furnished. We went into the den and I stood aside and watched as four people sat around a small round table and proceeded to make it tilt back and forth, answering various questions.

At first I was skeptical. It looked like they could be tilting the table with their fingers. But when it was my turn to sit in, I knew instantly this wasn't the case. The table moved with force and precision in unpredictable movements, so that our hands would nearly slip off the surface. It was obvious that there was some strange force at work here.

The table tilted up and down, rapping once for no and twice for yes, answering various questions of the sitters. I wasn't very impressed by the answers to the questions, and it reminded me of the child's toy, the *Magic 8-Ball*. The spirits tried to answer various questions, such as the number of keys in a person's pocket, but were incorrect in their responses.

Still I was very intrigued and asked Deborah if we could hold a few private sessions, just to study the limits of her ability.

Deborah happily agreed. In May of 1989, Christy and I returned to Deborah's house with tape recorder, camera, videotape, candles, compass, and plenty of pencils and paper. We were ready to see what Deborah could do with her strange talent.

We sat around the table and placed our hands on its surface. Instantly, it rose up on two legs. We then began to ask questions, trying to determine the identity of various spirits. The table would move with a different motion for each alleged spirit. However, none of the spirits were able to provide evidential information.

The table lifting method proved to be a difficult way to communicate information. After several efforts, it seemed a waste of energy to try and get any intelligible messages. Deborah admitted that she had found automatic writing to much more effective, and that she had gotten many personal messages which she believed to be authentically from her relatives.

We tried to get the spirits to move the compass needle, however, they were unable to do so. They were unable to guess the contents of closed envelopes, nor affect a candle flame. They were not able to produce any physical manifestation other than the table lifting.

The evening grew late, and we ended the experiment. However, one month later, Christy and I returned. This time we decided to focus not only Deborah's ability to transmit accurate information, but also her physical capacities.

First Deborah performed various automatic writing exercises during which loving messages came through from her relatives.

I suggested we make a Ouija board, which we did. Christy and I then each rested our fingers lightly on the pointer while Deborah continued automatic writing. The pointer moved around, spelling out numbers and letters seemingly at random. I wanted to try and contact my mother's spirit so I said, "Are you there mom!"

Suddenly, the pointer spelled out yes. Christy and I looked at each other in surprise. I said, "Is that you mom?"

"Yes."

I said, "What is the first thing you did when you died?"

The pointer quickly spelled out, "Saw phone." Now when I say the pointer spelled out, I mean that it sped across the paper and darted from letter to letter extremely quickly. It moved fast, just slow enough for us to read it, but too fast for us to be doing it ourselves.

*Saw phone?* I didn't even understand what that meant. I looked at Christy in confusion. I later recalled that she had died alone in her hotel bathroom, reaching for the phone.

"What was the second thing you did after you died?"

The pointer whipped out at high speed, faster than Christy or I could normally move it (we tried afterward). It spelled out one word: "Laughed."

"What was the third thing you did?"

"Took a nap."

"What was the fourth thing you did?"

"Saw God."

Christy and I looked at each other in shock. Then the pointer started swirling back and forth and started spelling out nonsense words again. That was all we could get out of it. While I do not know if we contacted my mother's spirit, I think it's definitely possible.

We then decided to focus on Deborah's ability as a physical medium. Just how much energy did it take to raise the table? Could she get it to actually levitate off the floor?

Deborah was able to do it alone. When Christy and I tried, neither of us could do it alone. We could, however, do it together without Deborah.

I then tried to do it myself and asked Deborah to lay her fingers as lightly as possible on the table. As soon as she did, the table promptly rose up to forty-five degrees.

I asked her to remove her hands from the table. After a few seconds, it fell back down. Still with my own hands lightly touching the table, I asked Deborah to touch the table with only one hand. She did so and the table quickly rose up.

I then asked her to repeat the experiment, but this time use only one finger. I was the only one touching the table and it wouldn't move. When Deborah lightly touched the table with her fingertip, it promptly rose up to forty-five degrees.

By now I was completely convinced that it was a real force we were dealing with here. I then tried one final time to make the table move by myself. I laid my fingers lightly on the table and asked in earnest for the spirits to make it move. To my amazement, the table shuddered back and forth, physically rocking and shaking several inches. It was definitely moving *by itself* under my fingertips. I was the only one touching the table, and it moved. Now I knew for sure. This was definitely real.

Although I couldn't get the table to go up, the feeling of the power pulsing underneath my hands was unmistakable. It felt like somebody had taken hold of the table and physically shaken it. And yet I was the only one touching it.

Now came the time to test the power of the spirits. I asked Deborah to make the table rise up and to ask the spirits to keep it there as firmly as possible while I tried to press it down physically.

Deborah made the table rise. I pressed down on it with my hand and was easily able to press it to the floor. I then held the table down and asked her to see if she could make it move. She was not able to do so.

Deborah was unable to make any rapping noises either. So we decided to try and make the table actually levitate. This was when things began to get even more interesting.

The three of us began chanting in earnest, "Up, table, up! Up, table, up!" over and over. The energy in the table began to change. The table itself became more and more active and bouncy, rocking back and forth. Normally it would tilt to a forty-five degree angle and stay there. As we chanted to it to levitate completely, it started walking back and forth across the room, bouncing from leg to leg. Then it began spinning in circles, forcing us to run around it breathlessly.

This went on for some time, then the table took on another movement where it would kind of skip across the floor in a gliding motion. We were all screaming and sweating in exhilaration.

The table would jump up for split seconds, and then thump back down. Still, it couldn't hold onto a full levitation. But we weren't about to give up and continued to ask the spirits to try and levitate the table.

Finally, it walked over to the downward staircase and tilted towards it. But instead of stopping at a forty five degree angle, it tilted to a completely horizontal position, over the open area where the steps went down. The only points of contact were two of the table legs on the edge of the top step. Then the table dipped down even farther and slowly lifted back up.

We all "oohed" and "ahhed" in amazement. Although the table didn't levitate fully, it was darn close.

This was all done in full light. There was absolutely no chance of trickery. Although we weren't able to get a full levitation, Deborah's spirits proved to Christy and me that they were very real indeed.

Today, Deborah rarely does any public sessions, and only does it once or twice a year. She has never charged a fee and has no plans to do it professionally.

Nevertheless, Deborah is a good example of a physical medium, which is the rarest type of medium. There are many famous mediums who can bring through evidential messages from the deceased. However, it is much rarer for someone to be able to produce physical manifestations.

Christy and I tried to repeat the experiment away from Deborah's house. We were successful at least once, but afterwards, it didn't work and after several repeated attempts, we gave up.

However, table lifting is easy to do and if the proper precautions are taken, it is totally safe. Deborah has done it for several years with few problems. Neither Christy nor I suffered any ill effects, other than perhaps some backlash from skeptics who had difficulty understanding our interest.

Table lifting is, like a Ouija board, easy access to the paranormal. It is a controlled haunting. A final warning for those who might attempt this, it is advised that it first be tried with someone who has done it before, or has experience with this type of thing. Although it may be easy to do, a controlled haunting can easily become an uncontrolled haunting overnight, leading to full-blown poltergeist infestation.

# 20 – The Wizard of Reseda

For most people, seeing a ghost is a rare experience. For some, however, it is anything but rare. For some unknown reason, an extremely small portion of the population sees ghosts regularly, even on a daily basis. Society recognizes these people as mediums.

Throughout history, the best mediums have often enjoyed celebrity status. This is because of their incredible ability to communicate with the deceased. A talented mental medium can sit next to a person and telepathically communicate with their deceased loved ones, providing names, dates, and specific details.

Skeptics often claim that mediums give general messages that would apply to any person, or that they read details by looking at the person, or asking the game of twenty questions.

However, the best mediums easily explode these theories. Currently, there are several famous mediums who have proven themselves to be genuine. People like Sylvia Brown, James Van Praagh, John Edward, Rosemary Altea, George Anderson, and many others have convinced countless people of their ability to talk to the dead. Each of them have waiting lists that are years long.

Another medium of equal caliber to the above select group is a man by the name of Brian Hurst. Born in England in 1938, like most great mediums, he had many early experiences with ghosts. As a child, he saw apparitions, and heard strange voices whispering messages in his head. At night, his bedroom would become crowded with ghosts.

It all began after he was nearly electrocuted at the tender age of seven. Many psychics report the start of their psychic abilities following a traumatic near-death experience. Brian's case fits the model perfectly. He stuck a metal object in an electrical socket and received a powerful jolt of electricity. Following that, he began to see ghosts. As Brian writes in his excellent autobiography, *Heaven Can Help,* "Shortly after that experience I remember having strange dreams in which I was floating out of my body and swimming through a rainbow of colours....Sometimes I would hear voices speaking to me in the darkness and see strange faces floating about in the air....Looking back, I really believe that the strong electric shock I received may well have been responsible for the opening up of my psychic awareness."

However, Brian was probably already destined to be a medium, for even as a baby of eighteen months, he attracted ghosts. As his mother reports, "Suddenly as I looked in your [Brian's] direction I saw this dark misty shape suddenly appear beside your cot....I stared at this strange shape at the foot of the bed and I remember thinking for a moment that someone must have crept into the room while I wasn't looking. I almost expected to be attacked, but then to my amazement the shape raised an arm and pointed at you lying in your cot fast asleep."

Shortly later, the apparition disappeared. Brian's mother was left only with the feeling that her child was fated for something unusual.

She was right. As he grew older, Brian began to see more ghosts. Following the death of his grandfather, he experienced several sightings of his spirit. "Every night when the lights were turned out I would see grandfather standing there, looking at me with his pale blue eyes. Sometimes he would try to touch me and I would dive under the bedclothes. I knew that he should be in Heaven and I could never understand at that time why he kept coming to visit me. I believe these manifestations were an early sign of my mediumship."

More and more strange events began to occur. He and his childhood best friend used to play games with telepathy. They found it worked best when Brian was the receiver. "Repeatedly I was able to describe his thoughts in detail, and he was quite amazed by my accuracy. This was all very new and exciting."

For the first time, Brian found that there was some use for his strange abilities. "I frequently heard voices in my head, a few of which gave me helpful directions, like telling me the location of mushrooms in the fields."

While the voices weren't always helpful, and sometimes taunted him, Brian was beginning to realize that all of this wasn't in his head, it was real.

By coincidence, Brian attended a series of séances and became increasingly interested in spiritualism. He developed his talent quietly. Then one day, he was conversing with a friend when he clearly saw the image of a man with a bushy mustache floating above her head. The name "Georgie" popped into his mind. He described what he was seeing to his friend when she smiled widely and said, "That's my father you're describing!"

His friend was so delighted, she insisted that he do public readings. So began his formal mediumship. He not only trained in private circles, he visited numerous other famous mediums. He observed all kinds of phenomena from apparitions, ghostly voices, phantom touches, levitation of objects and even of people!

At this time, he didn't give public readings, and worked as a teacher. His students soon learned of his perceptive abilities. "While teaching I was often able to surprise some of the children by my knowledge of events around them, simply by holding on to their pens or books. On one occasion I told a child that I thought her mother's friend had won some money at Bingo. She absolutely denied this, but on returning to school the next day she informed me with utter amazement that what I had predicted had occurred that very evening. Several children in the class said that I must be a kind of wizard, and I was known by some of the more intelligent children as the 'telepathic teacher.' One tall, troubled boy of fifteen said I gave him the creeps when I mentioned that he had just had a new red lampshade put in his bedroom."

In 1973, he left England for a teaching job in India. He spent a few years teaching there, then returned to England. Feeling restless, in 1980 he decided to move to California, and settled in the community of Reseda.

There his reputation as an accurate mental medium began to spread. He never did any advertising. He worked initially only with friends. But through word of mouth, he soon had a waiting list months in advance. This led to a number of appearances in the media. During this time, he met a young man named James Van Praagh and gave him the reading which would change his life. Brian told James that he had the potential to be an excellent medium and encouraged him to develop his ability. James Van Praagh is now, like Hurst, a world-famous medium.

Hurst's claim to fame is simple: he is incredibly accurate. After many years of doing readings, he has developed his talent to a miraculous degree. Through the help of his spirit guide, Doctor Grant, he is not only able to talk to the dead, but can also give psychic readings, health readings, and predictions.

I first heard about Brian Hurst through a friend. Later, while reading James Van Praagh's book, I learned that Praagh credited Hurst with awakening his own ability. By researching on the internet, I found that Brian Hurst lived in Reseda, only a few miles from my own home! And furthermore, he held monthly meetings.

While most great mediums charge exorbitant fees (and still have long waiting lists), Brian's fees are miniscule in comparison.

I called up and made a reservation.

Having watched such television programs like *Beyond With James Van Praagh,* and *Crossing Over With John Edward*, I was basically familiar with the technique of mediumship.

When I arrived, a small group had already gathered outside and were waiting to enter. I made careful notes of their conversations to make sure that Mr. Hurst wouldn't just regurgitate the information. None of it was.

We were invited in. Several chairs had been set up in the living room. By the time the meeting was ready to start, about forty people were present. Hurst began the evening with a lecture about mediumship. Then after a short break, he began.

He started with a short meditation. Then tilting his head, he began to look around the room. I must say that what happened next shocked me so much that I didn't keep careful notes.

He pointed to a lady and began to list of a string of personal details about her that he couldn't have possibly known. Her only response was yes, yes, yes.

He turned to another and told him details about his deceased father, about his childhood, his ancestry and other personal details.

One after another, he would pick someone out of the audience and rattle off various facts. These were not generalizations, but specific facts. I tried to make the readings fit my own life, but none did.

Hurst read twelve people in all, and then ended the evening.

I was disappointed I didn't get a reading, but was determined to try again. Brian only holds public meetings once a month, so I had to wait.

The second meeting was the same. He gave readings to about one-third of the audience members. He tilted his head and said, "I don't know what this means, but I'm seeing a pots and pans. Do you understand this?" The person being read said without hesitation, "I'm a cook."

He turned to another person and asked her if there was a history of diabetes in her family. Yes, came the answer. Then followed about five more minutes of incredible revelations about her deceased loved ones.

The spirits were evidently careful to provide information that proves their existence of life after death.

All these readings were incredible, but I couldn't know for sure until I received my own reading.

While it didn't happen on that night, I attended the next month. To my delight, Brian pointed to me and said, "I see books above your head. Do you have any connection with science-fiction?"

"Yes," I answered. As a teen-ager, I read every science fiction book I could get my hands on.

"Because I see science-fiction books around you. Authors like Arthur C. Clark, Robert Heinlein, Ray Bradbury."

"Yes," I replied. "I've read all those authors."

Then he tilted his head again and said, "Do you do writing?"

"Yes," I replied.

"Because the spirits are telling me that you do writing. You have a lot of creative ideas. They're telling me they like what you are doing and you will get published."

"I just found out yesterday that I sold a piece."

Everybody laughed and clapped.

Brian said, "See, I didn't know that. I don't know you. I see you writing many different things, maybe even something to do with this subject."

"Yes, that's true."

Mr. Hurst then skipped over and gave a reading to my sister-in-law, sitting next to me. He connected to her grandmother and mentioned that she and Christy used to polish the silverware together. Christy gasped in recognition. He then listed a few other details which were verified, then seemed to lose his connection with her.

I attended the next month and to my amazement, Brian again picked me out of the audience. He obviously didn't recognize me as he sees a constant parade of thousands of people through his home. He said, "You're just dying for a reading, aren't you."

"Me? Yes," I replied. I was.

"I feel you have a great tremendous interest and curiosity about all this. You're just really fired up about all this."

"Yes, that's true."

"Well, this may sound a little strange, but I see a small plane above your head...either a model plane or a small Cessna. Does that make any sense?"

"Yes," I replied. "My father flies a small plane."

"Is he deceased?"

"No."

"I'm getting a grandfatherly feeling. I think this is his father. I don't mean to embarrass you."

"Go right ahead."

"But did your grandfather have more hair than you?"

I laughed. "I don't know." I am losing my hair rapidly. I later found out my grandfather always had a full head of hair.

He asked then if I had Scotch/Irish background. I am one quarter Irish, but not Scottish.

At this point, Brian seemed to be pulled to another person. He mentioned painting Easter eggs, a connection to Phoenix, Arizona and Laughlin, Nevada. None of this rang a bell with me, but a lady one row ahead of me began to fidget and then called out, "That's me." She turned around and apologized to me, but then explained to everyone that she has a strong connection to Laughlin and a Scottish background. Brian apologized that sometimes the communication gets garbled between two spirits.

He asked me, "Is David dead? Do you know a David?"

"Not dead," I replied. "I know a David, yes."

"Does your father know, him?"

"No." It looked like Brian was getting off track again. At that point, however, he made another incredible hit.

"Did your father recently build a small shed outside his home?"

"Yes," I replied, amazed. He had set up the shed a few months earlier.

"I also see someone in your family who is doing a lot of rebuilding, sawing, and putting up fences, redoing the house, painting. Does that make sense?"

"Yes." My brother had just repainted his kitchen and put up a new fence. He is *always* doing *something* to improve his home.

"You know I wouldn't be surprised if somebody built their own house somewhere, in sectional homes." My brother did exactly that, and our family has a dream of living somewhere on a large piece of land with neighboring but separate homes. It appeared Brian had picked up on this too.

"Buy a piece of land, buy a bunch of sectional homes and put the houses together."

"Yes, I'd love to do that."

"Yeah, I think you would. That would be a challenge for you, wouldn't it? Your grandfather is aware of this. It looks like it's on the horizon, in the future, something to do with building a sectional home, putting it all together, getting a team of people working together. Like a family, building the house together. I don't know where it would be built."

We had always hoped for a nice place outside of Los Angeles. Christy often mentioned Merced county.

"Have you heard of an area called San Luis Obispo, central California, south of Merced?"

"Yes, actually. We were thinking of that." He hit the area exactly.

"Your grandfather has been aware of your thoughts and aware of your plans, what you. He wishes you all the success. Was there anybody called Gordon?"

In couldn't think of any Gordon. Later, I recalled that my father's next door neighbor who had died had that name, but that seemed kind of a reach.

"Lord Gordon."

"No."

"Do you have a connection to Colorado?"

"No, well I know someone there."

"Well, you may visit Colorado, that's all I can tell you."

At this point, Brian went to another person.

A third reading with Brian was equally impressive. Although this time he remembered me, again, he didn't seem to recall any details about my life. "Somebody says something about Preston having an interest in science fiction or science fantasy at one time."

"Yes, that's very true."

"And having a collection of Isaac Asimov, Arthur C. Clarke, and all these kind of science-fiction fantasy writers, Ray Bradbury, and you were a connoisseur of that kind of thing."

"Yes, I read all those authors." So far this was repetitive, but still accurate.

"Have you thought about trying to write something like that?"

"Absolutely, I am a writer."

"I see writing, with you Preston. Haven't you had some stuff published?"

"Yes, I do paranormal stuff."

"Scott Rogo and Raymond Bayless wrote a book, *Phone Call from the Dead*. Do you have that?"

"Yes." A good hit.

"You have a big collection like me, you've got a big collection of books on this subject."

"Yes, huge." Another hit.

"They tell me about *Fate* magazine. Have you written for *Fate* magazine?"

"Yes, I have. I just got an article published."

"Well that's factual. They told me, 'He's got an article in Fate.'"

"That is true."

"I feel sort of embarrassed about this. But somebody says you're going to write about me later on?"

I laughed. I had told nobody, but again he was correct. I definitely wanted to write about him. "I wanted to ask you about that, actually. I was going to ask you tonight."

Brian continued the reading, saying I would have a long life. He mentioned that I was very different from my brothers, which is also true. At this point, the reading seemed to flounder. He named a few names I didn't recognize and then shifted to another person.

He also gave my sister-in-law Christy another reading. She was in tears by the end of the reading. As she says, "He was pretty right on, and I felt the people he was talking about near me. It was all verified. He's doing a really wonderful service for people because losing loved ones can be a real grievous experience, and for him to be able to communicate with them is such a relief to the people who are grieving."

Although Brian does make some mistakes in his readings, the majority of what he says is correct. I analyzed several other readings of his. In one case, he stated more than forty specific names and facts, all of which were confirmed correct by the amazed sitter. Only four or five details elicited a negative response.

Brian himself is often confused about the information coming through to him simply because he has no idea what it means. As he jokingly says, "I really do make a living not knowing what I'm talking about."

But those who are listening to him do know what he's talking about.

Brian Hurst's case is important because it shows that people can and do interact with ghosts safely, easily, and regularly. His case removes the fear of encountering ghosts and facing death. Through his readings, he is able to lift some of the mystery surrounding the subject of the other side, and alleviate the suffering caused by the loss of loved ones.

# 21 – The Legacy of the Charles Manson Murders

It is well-known that tragic deaths can cause a home or place to become haunted. What is not as well known is that an act of evil can also bring about a haunting. Many people who have severely haunted homes later discover that horrific acts have occurred there such as satanic sacrifices, black magic, murders, suicides, acts of sexual perversion, devil worshipping, or some other awful event. These types of hauntings can be distinguished from others by their particularly evil nature.

In the 1970s, the city of Los Angeles was gripped in terror by the hideous crimes of Charles Manson. He and his gang went on a spree of murders that shocked the nation. Manson was eventually apprehended by the police. He was put on trial, found guilty of murder, and imprisoned.

The evil nature of his crimes made a lasting impression on the public. However, what is not as well known is that his crimes have left a trail of haunted houses – homes that were forever changed by the events that occurred there.

Margaret Patterson (not her real name) has been a real-estate agent for over twenty-five years. She had heard about the murders, but never really paid much attention to them. But then, her job as a real-estate agent brought her right to the door of one of the houses where the Manson gang had committed a ghastly crime.

It all began when a lady came into the office looking for a home in the Santa Monica mountains. As Margaret says, "I worked in real-estate and this woman came into my office and she wanted to buy a house. I asked her how much she could spend. I don't know what it was, but it was like twelve thousand dollars or fourteen thousand dollars. Most of the houses were going for about twenty-five thousand then. That was probably like the early seventies.

"I didn't have anything and she went on and on about how she just wanted a place that was habitable and she didn't care all that much about it. She wasn't fussy, and she only wanted to be here in the canyon, and on and on. She reminded me of a gypsy-type lady, overweight with a muumuu on, a fortune-teller type, you know what I mean?

"So finally, she kept pushing, and there was this one house that we had that was vacant. They were asking thirteen-five. It was very small. It was a one bedroom, almost a tree-house type little affair, among the trees. I had never been into it before, but it was on the market. We had a key in the office.

"So I said, 'There is this one place. It needs a whole lot of work and so forth, but if you're not fussy and all, I'll show it to you.'

"So she got in the car and we drove up there. She was really excited. She just said, 'This is going to be perfect. Everything is great.' We parked in front; it was up on the side of a hill. You had to walk up a lot of wooden steps to get to it, and you entered on the balcony. And she said, 'Oh, it's so beautiful. There's oak trees. This is just terrific.' And so on and so forth.

"So we got there and I opened the door. We went in. We saw that it was vacant. She just started wandering around. It wasn't all that big. I just sort of stood there. I hadn't been in it before. And after about three minutes, she began to sort of change. She said, 'Something's going on here.' And she didn't wait for me to answer. She said, 'Gee, I'm feeling something. I feel something. It feels heavy in here. What is it? I don't know what it is.' She said, 'I'm not feeling good about this.' She said it was heavy. She kept going on. She said, 'Something's happened here. Did something happen here?' And she went on and on.

"So the thing that I knew ahead of time – and I wasn't going to tell her; I didn't know how to deal with it actually, but I decided I wouldn't say anything to her about this particular house. Because I never have to talk about it because she might not like the house. And if she did like it, I would have to tell her. But the bottom line was, this was the house that Charlie Manson murdered somebody in. And she picked up the vibes on it. And I didn't tell her anything. I'm sure she didn't set me up to do that kind of thing. She picked up on some kind of energy that was happening there. I couldn't believe that she was picking this up."

The lady kept on talking about something evil having happened there so Margaret eventually told her the truth. Needless to say, the lady didn't buy the house.

Today there is a disclosure law requiring real-estate agents to reveal if a murder has occurred in the house. Back then, however, there was no disclosure law. Margaret was stunned that the lady was able to somehow sense the fact that something bad had happened there.

She was glad that she was under no obligation to try and get the house sold. Eventually the house was sold. The new owners remodeled and expanded the home. Margaret does not know if the new residents have experienced any activity.

That house, however, is not the only house to have become haunted after a Manson murder had occurred. Another much larger house in the Hollywood Hills was the location of another of the Manson killings. It was in this house that Sharon Tate's life was forever ended.

The house, which was a normal happy household before the incident, soon started to change. Strange incidents began to occur. An evil presence began to make itself known.

Sarah Webster is a pilot, flight instructor, and gardener from Los Angeles, California. By mere coincidence, Sarah happened to know somebody who had a connection with the murders. As Sarah says, "A friend of mine's grandmother is very good friends with the man who actually owned the house that the Tate-La Bianca murders happened in. He was going off to Europe for a few years or something like that, I don't know exactly how long. But when he was leaving, Sharon Tate begged him to let her stay in his house while he was gone. And with a lot of misgivings, he let her do it. And that's where she got killed by the Manson crew, and a whole bunch of other people got killed by the Manson crew.

"I went there with the granddaughter of the woman who knew this guy. And we went there in the evening. We were going to have dinner there. And we got there. It was a beautiful house built up in the Hollywood Hills, a gorgeous view. And my friend was saying, 'You really ought to see the rest of the house.' And I said, 'Okay.'

"It was getting dark and the owner of the house was cooking dinner, and he said, 'Go ahead, check it out.' And we started wandering around and we would try all of the light switches and nothing would work. One of us would stand at the light switch and the other one would be at the lamp trying it in different ways and we couldn't get any of the lights to turn on at all through the entire house. And the owner came in, and he would flip the exact same switches that we had done, and it would work. It was really blowing my mind particularly after about the third or fourth time he did it. And then we went wandering into the back of the house.

"And in this back bedroom, actually in the bathroom in the back bedroom – that was the first place we could actually turn on the lights, which was another weird thing. We're like, 'Wow, check it out,' And it was just crawling with flies. It was just *filled* with flies. It felt like something out of a Hitchcock movie. There were thousands of them. They were everywhere. It was like everywhere you looked. They were all over the mirrors, all over the counters, all over the ceilings. It was really disgusting. We screamed and ran.

"It just really spooked us after the whole light experience and knowing about the murders having happened there. We beat a hasty retreat out of there and pretty much left as soon as we could, feeling very spooked by the whole thing."

Both Sarah and her friend ran breathlessly down the stairs and confronted the owner. They told him everything, about how the lights hadn't worked except in the bathroom which was all filled with flies. The owner just shrugged and casually, "Yeah, I've been having problems with that room."

Sarah didn't bother to ask him if he had experienced any other ghostly activity. As she says, "I did not ask him about that. It was kind of a touchy subject for him. He didn't really like the fact that a murder had happened in his house."

Sarah and her friend ate dinner quickly and politely left as soon as they could. Since then, they have never been back. The property was later sold, and the new owners completely tore down the house and built a brand new home.

Sarah reports that although the experience was somewhat frightening, she was intrigued by the experience and wishes that other people could know what it's like to be in a haunted house. As she says, "Really it was a stunning house, other than these small problems with the light switches and the bugs. It was more disturbing than scary. I definitely felt like there was some type of otherworldly presence of some kind or another. But I didn't feel personally threatened. I think it was kind of neat. I mean, we need to have haunted houses."

As can be seen, Charles Manson's crimes definitely left a strong impression on the homes in which they were perpetrated. Most of the manifestations are somewhat common. For example, a sense of an evil presence and lights going on and off by themselves are not unusual manifestations. A very unusual manifestation is the flies which filled the bathroom. This has appeared in only a few of the most severe cases of hauntings, and yet, it is a detail that has been repeated.

Whatever the case, the phenomenon is real, and in the above cases, seems to be the result not of the spirits of those people who were killed, but by the violent and evil nature of the acts of murder. In both cases the hauntings were stopped after the houses were either remodeled or torn down and rebuilt. In both cases, the houses experienced no activity until the murders occurred.

This case is interesting not only because of the notoriety the murders received, but because they clearly illustrate the consequences of evil acts, such as murder. An evil act can literally cause a house to become infested by evil spirits. And because the Manson murders were particularly evil, they left a haunted legacy that lasted for many years.

# 22 – A Demon Named Bart

Many troublesome haunting cases begin when someone opens a spiritual doorway, often through the indiscriminate use of a Ouija board. In the following case, three sisters and a friend invited a spirit into their home through this innocent-looking board game.

The girls lived with their parents in their home in Malibu, California. They lived a normal childhood, going to school, making friends, doing their chores, playing games. One day in 1975, they began to experiment with the Ouija board.

At first it was fun. They took a piece of paper and wrote down the alphabet and numbers. Then they took a penny and each of them put one finger on it. To their surprise and delight, the penny moved and spelled out intelligible messages. As Jennifer, the youngest sister says, "We would do this every so often. We would make a Ouija board out of a sheet of paper and a copper penny. And we were so young, I don't think any of us were up to pranks. It seemed so real that it was happening. There was no questioning it. We were these young kids, and we were like playing with this stuff, and it was all kind of happening."

Kelly, the middle sister, became intrigued with the idea of contacting the spirits of famous people. "I don't know what got me hooked on Jack Benny when I was little," she explains, "but I just tried so hard to contact him. He was my favorite. And I know I used to contact someone that used to *respond* to Jack Benny. I don't know if it was him or not, but I thought it was. Agnes Moorhead was another one of my favorites, when I was little. We just tried to reach people like that...we played with the Ouija board so much when we were little and never had the problem of running into something that was scary."

The three sisters spent many hours sitting around the Ouija board, trying to contact various spirits. Then one night in 1975, they and their friend, Amy, had a frightening encounter with a bad ghost. Jennifer was six years old, Kelly was nine, and Amy was twelve. Her friend Heidi was also twelve.

They gathered together on the outside deck and drew up one of their homemade Ouija boards. They all sat around and put a finger on the penny. First, they tried to contact Jack Benny. As Kelly says, "I thought that I had had success in reaching him before. I don't know. I mean, I don't why the hell Jack Benny would be wanting to talk to me. But we were definitely going in that direction of trying to reach him."

Normally the Ouija board would spell out, "Hello," and give various puzzling messages. This time, however, it did something very different. Says Jennifer, "We were all excited and started asking questions. Anyway, it just started to not give us answers, or not the answers we were looking for. It started jumbling words, letters and words…the penny would go really fast off the paper. You'd have your finger on it, and it would move quickly off the paper either with your finger, or leaving it behind. It never flew off the table or anything, but it would just move across the paper."

The four young girls looked at each in confusion. Why wasn't the Ouija board behaving? They continued probing the spirit, trying to get coherent answers about who it was. They were not at all prepared for what it was about to tell them. Says Kelly, "What I remember was that we made a Ouija board out of paper and then we were trying to just get anybody to communicate with us. So we weren't very careful. We just opened it up to whoever wanted to come in and talk to us. It was fine. We thought we were going to try to go for certain people that we wanted to talk to, but we weren't getting any response. And then, all of a sudden, it started moving around. It wouldn't give us who it was, but it kept saying that it was really close. And we knew by asking it, 'Are you in our house?'

"And it said it was in the house, and it wouldn't give us any name. But it wasn't very friendly. I just remember it not being terribly friendly. It was kind of hostile or aggressive. I don't even remember the questions that we asked it. But I do remember we got really scared because it said it was in the house. Why we were scared, I don't know – if it told us that it was mean or not…I know we talked to it for a while. I don't remember the specifics, but for some reason, we got the impression that this thing was not a nice spirit. That's why we were scared of it…It started moving and all of a sudden, it was like I didn't know who we were dealing with. And we made him spell out his name and it was just scary. It turned scary solely through whatever this thing was saying to us, because we had done it enough times where it wasn't scary. It wasn't like we were scared to begin doing it."

Jennifer also remembers the spirit saying that it was in the house, and like the other girls, she was anxious to know exactly who it was. It seemed pretty obvious that it wasn't Agnes Moorhead or Jack Benny. The spirit kept avoiding revealing its name and kept saying it was close by, in the house. The girls were insistent, however, and demanded that the spirit reveal who it was. Finally, the spirit spelled out its name. All four girls became instantly terrified.

Says Jennifer, "It started jumbling letters and words. It was definitely playing with us, scaring us. And then whoever we were speaking with just told us that we were talking to someone related to Satan, and that his name was Bart, and he was a demon. And obviously, it totally freaked us out. We were all really terrified. The thing that was so weird – and I remember all these things so clearly because we were so terrified – I remember he said he was a demon. I think at first he was saying he was Satan. And we were asking about him about that and being afraid, and then he divulged that he was a demon and he gave his name. It was really kind of strange."

At this point the four girls were literally trembling with fear. Had they invited the Devil himself into their home? It didn't seem possible. But worst of all, the spirit kept saying that he was in the house waiting for them. It was Heidi who finally hit upon a plan of action. Says Jennifer, "What ended up happening is, he said he was in our house. And Heidi told us that the only way to get rid of the spirit is to burn the Ouija board or piece of paper. So my older sister, Amy, was hysterical and grabbed me. And we went outside and grabbed one of the dogs."

The four of them decided that Kelly would go inside the house and get matches to burn the Ouija board. They had several dogs, and one of them was a young Doberman named Gandolph. As soon as Kelly opened the door, Gandolph ran excitedly into the house and started barking furiously at somebody or something. Kelly ran after the dog. She had no idea she was about to come face-to-face with the ghost.

Says Kelly, "We decided we had to burn the Ouija board. This is what our friend said. We had to get rid of the spirit and just break the connection that we had invited to have in our house. So somebody had to go inside and get matches. So I was volunteered, I don't know why. And I took our dog. We went past the sliding glass door and the dog took off down the hall, barking. And I went running after it, calling it. And the dog was going absolutely ballistic, barking and screaming and looking up at the stairway. There was nobody there. There was nobody home except us kids."

Kelly ran to the foot of the stairs and grabbed Gandolph. Looking up, she got the shock of her life. "I saw a shadow or *something* in the stairway. I don't know. It was pretty spooky. It was just a grayish – I mean, something moved. It was not necessarily a figure I could make out. There was something that moved along the wall. I don't know what I was seeing. The dog and I were looking at the same area. So I finally got the dog under control and went flying out of the house with some matches. I have no idea what the dog was barking at. We burned the Ouija board and basically stayed under the house until my mom got home."

Jennifer's account agrees with her sisters'. "The dog ran down the hallway and just started turning circles and barking at the end of the hallway. And Kelly ran into the house to get some matches. And Kelly swears that she thought she saw a shadow or something while she was trying to grab the dog. She was trying to get the dog, to get the dog's attention and leave the house. She got the matches and ran out of the house. We burned the Ouija board. And we just sat outside and my mom came home."

When their mom came home and found them all cowering under the house in fear, she naturally wondered what had scared them so badly. The girls quickly spilled out their story. Says Kelly, "She came in and walked around the house and there was nothing. And the dog was fine. When we walked back in the house, it kind of walked around. We took it right to the stairway, and nothing. So I have no clue what was going on. I don't know what led it down the hallway to bark other than thinking there was something there."

While Jennifer's terror caused her to remember the incident in vivid detail, Kelly tried to shove the incident out of her mind. "I don't have a real vivid memory because of the dog situation and being in the house pretty much scared me to death. So about all I remember from that day is being the one suckered to go inside."

After that incident, their mother sat them all down and explained to them about the spirit world. As it turned out, their family had a rich history of ghost encounters, and some family members had varying degrees of mediumistic talent.

In the past, their mother Ardelle had several experiences with ghosts, so she had no doubt they were real. Luckily, the girls' terrifying encounter appeared to be an isolated experience.

However, later, Ardelle experienced a frightening introduction in her Malibu home involving a bad ghost. She admits that at the time, she had been using the Ouija board frequently. Whether or not what happened next is related to the girls' experience is hard to say.

Ardelle went to bed normally, but in the middle of the night, someone or something woke her up and tried to pull her out of bed. Says Ardelle, "I was alone in the house. I was upstairs in my bedroom in bed, and all of a sudden, something, somebody was trying to pull me out of bed. I remember grabbing onto the sheets and yelling. I had a Doberman at the time – she must have been about eleven when this happened. She was asleep at the end of the hall. I remember she was a very sound sleeper. At that point I had been delving into psychic phenomena and I immediately figured that somebody was trying to make contact with me. But I couldn't understand why I was being pulled out of bed. I said, 'Get your hands off of me!'

"I remember I held onto the sheet and was grabbing at the bed so that I wouldn't be pulled onto the floor. And that was so distinct. What I felt was like two hands pulling at me, like somebody had the back of my nightgown or something, and was pulling me. They were not actually touching me; they weren't pinching me. But they were actually pulling my bedclothes to pull me out of bed. And I was holding on. Finally I just yelled, 'Let me alone!!!'

"And the whole thing, whatever the force was, just totally disintegrated. And I sat up, turned on the lights and went through the whole house. When I got up, of course my dog went with me. We turned all the lights on inside and out. I didn't see anything. I couldn't understand it. It was so real. It was more like I thought there was somebody, maybe like a robber or somebody in the house with me. But I couldn't understand how they could have gotten by my dog."

Ardelle was frightened by the encounter, but assumed the incident was over. However, a few weeks later, she had another experience that was equally bizarre. She was again alone in the house when she distinctly heard somebody calling her name.

Says Ardelle, "It was coming from the front of the house, by my front door. It was not a voice I remember. It was just somebody saying, 'Ardelle! Ardelle! Ardelle!' And at that point, by the third time, I was running towards the front hall. Our neighbor on one side is very ill and her husband has called me on occasion to come help. And I thought maybe somehow that was it, and he was yelling at my front door so frantically that I heard. I didn't feel any coldness. I didn't feel anything. I got to the stairwell, looking downstairs at my front door, didn't see anything, walked downstairs, walked around the house, did the whole go around. I didn't see anything. I didn't hear anything. I went back and sat in bed, totally confused."

This case is typical of what can happen when people use a Ouija board. It appears that the ghost was able to manifest more easily when people used the Ouija board. However, the family had used the Ouija board for years without ill effects. Further questioning also revealed that Ardelle and Kelly had a number of other psychic experiences, such as precognition or out-of-body experiences.

Fortunately, they have suffered no further negative encounters. However, with their history, it is likely they will see ghosts again.

# 23 – A House Possessed

Diane Robinson (pseudonym) was born in the 1930s in New Jersey. She grew up as a tomboy, doing her best to keep up with her older brother and his friends as they explored the fields behind their rural home.

Diane has always believed in ghosts because when she was only thirteen years old, she had the first of what was to be a life-long series of ghost encounters. She was visiting her aunt's house and was in the bathroom brushing her teeth when she distinctly heard a loud moaning sound next to her. She ran in terror into the hallway, and as she did so, the attic door opened and closed by itself.

Diane stopped, turned around and bravely climbed up the stairs towards the attic door. To her surprise, she saw that an object had been placed midway on the stairs. It was her grandmother's ceramic swan that was supposed to go to Diane's mother, but had been hidden by the aunt.

Throughout the years, Diane had other psychic experiences including a near-death experience following dental surgery, precognitive dreams, and clairvoyant visions. In the late 1960s, she and her husband moved to North Hollywood, California. Her husband worked in the military and she continued working as a secretary.

Directly behind the Robinsons lived a sweet, old Mexcian lady. Even though she was ninety years old, she was always active and cheerful. Unfortunately she did not know how to speak English, so she and Diane were nothing more than casual friends. But every morning when Diane went outside to hang her laundry, her neighbor would be there tending her roses, smiling and singing Mexican lullabies. Each time they saw each other, they would say good morning which, due to the language barrier, was all they could say.

Says Diane, "I went out one morning and I was hanging up clothes and I heard her singing. And I heard her say, 'Good morning,' I went over to the fence to smile at her and and say good morning back, but there was nothing, no one – no one was there. I walked along the fence because she couldn't move that fast; she was very old. And she wasn't there. The phone was ringing in the house and I picked up the phone in the kitchen. And it was her granddaughter, and her granddaughter said, 'I just wanted to tell you that my grandmother passed away this morning. She had pneumonia and she passed away.'"

Other incidents like that proved to Diane that she had some mediumistic ability. But it was something she usually kept quiet. She and her husband just continued to live a normal life. They gave birth to two girls, Jenny and three years later, Kelly (pseudonyms), and started saving to buy a home.

The children grew up quickly. Little incidents occurred throughout the years, but it was on Kelly's tenth birthday that something happened which proved conclusively that Diane had mediumistic ability.

On a whim, Diane and Kelly and her friends at the party decided to try and communicate with spirits. Diane was only half-joking as they all sat around a small table and laid their hands on the surface.

Suddenly, Diane felt a strange powerful force move through her body and the table instantly lifted all four legs off the floor and levitated several inches off the floor. Kelly and her friends jumped back screaming and the table fell. Kelly looked at her mother and said, "Mom, are we witches?" Diane assured her daughter that they were not.

However, Diane was stunned. She had definitely felt some sort of force move into her body. She vowed never to fool around with anything like table-lifting again.

They quickly forgot about the incident and life went back to normal. A few years later, Diane and her husband finally had enough money to buy a house of their own. They found a little house in Reseda, a densely populated suburb in the San Fernando Valley outside of Los Angeles, California. The house was very inexpensive and both Diane and her husband liked it right away. They made plans to buy the house. Within a month, they moved in.

The house had two bedrooms and a den, perfect for their two teenage daughters. It wasn't brand new. An elderly retired couple owned it previously. The husband had died several years ago at work. Then the wife became ill and expired in the hospital. The house was put up for sale and the Robinsons moved in.

Almost immediately, Diane began to notice strange things about the house. They were just odd occurrences that most people would pass off as meaningless. The first clue that the house was haunted came in the form of an unexplained odor. Several times Diane would walk into a room and smell the distinct odor of cigar smoke. Each time she would check to see if the windows were open or if the smell was coming from outside or another room. But the odor was always very localized and would quickly dissipate. Sometimes, however, it was so strong that Diane was sure somebody had just smoked a cigar in the room.

She just shrugged the incidents off and busied herself moving into the house, unpacking boxes, arranging the furniture. The house was everything they had hoped.

Then, a few months after they moved in, they were woken up one night by the sound of something crashing downstairs. It sounded to Diane like dishes falling or tables tipping over. They ran downstairs, but were unable to find the source of the noise. Nothing was out of order.

Over the next few weeks, this happened four or five times. On each occasion, they would run downstairs, absolutely sure that something had broken. But nothing ever was. Dan dismissed the incidents as nothing more than odd, however, Diane was beginning to suspect that something was amiss.

Besides the strange odors and unexplainable noises, she noticed another event that occurred shortly after they moved in. "When we used to have company and we would be out on the back porch, we would hear footsteps in the house. Although the front door was locked and there was no entry, someone would be in the house. And then we'd hear the toilet flush maybe once or twice and we'd come in and there was nobody in the house – not a soul in the house. And yet we had all heard the footsteps in the house."

The ghost began to show itself more and more openly. Says Diane, "When we first moved in here, I was ironing in the kitchen. We have an ironing board that comes down out of the wall, and there's a den door. As I was ironing, I was looking right at the den door. And the door slammed shut with a bang. It scared the wits out of me. So I opened the door again and I went and did something else. And I came back in the kitchen and the door slammed shut on me again. It was strange."

Diane insists that it wasn't a breeze which shut the door. It was slammed shut twice, just as if somebody had violently pushed it.

Needless to say, she was becoming concerned. All of her previous experiences with ghosts had involved the friendly spirits of her relatives or friends, and each experience was isolated and purposeful. This new ghost, however, was somehow different. Not only did she have no idea who it was, this ghost wasn't going away.

In fact, it was only getting stronger. Although they had only moved in a few months ago, the Robinsons had already experienced a wide variety of phenomena including unexplained odors, noises, footsteps, self-flushing toilets, and doors that close by themselves.

Diane decided that their house must be haunted. Shortly after she had this realization, the haunting seemed to escalate.

It all started with a missing pair of keys. The ghost or poltergeist, was becoming mischievous. It also marked the first time that the ghost exhibited itself in front of the children.

Says Diane, "Jenny wanted her bicycle out of the garage. We had the key hanging up in the kitchen here. She had three friends in the kitchen at the time besides me, and we were all in the kitchen standing around. Jenny reached for the key and the key fell to the kitchen floor. We all heard it. We all saw it fall in the vicinity that it fell, and we heard it hit the floor. And Jenny looked down and the key was not there. So she says, 'The key isn't there!'

"So we're all down looking for the keys. And while we're down on our hands and knees crawling around the floor looking for the key, the back door opened and shut twice!"

If the ghost was trying to scare them, then it worked. Diane reports that she was definitely frightened. The worst part for her, however, was that Dan remained skeptical. Says Diane, "When Dan came home from work, he thought we were all crazy, because nobody had picked up the key. It was nowhere in the kitchen and to this day, we never found the key to the garage. The kids were so scared that they ran out of here. That was the weirdest thing. Dan thought I was nuts. Jenny said, 'We heard it hit the floor, Dad.' And then it wasn't there. And then the back door opened and shut, twice, slammed.'"

Dan was still unbelieving, but now Diane was sure they had a ghost, and Jenny was also convinced. Diane didn't tell the children about the other things that had happened because she didn't want to scare them. She was sure, however, that their house was definitely haunted.

Thankfully the activity seemed to die down. In fact, several years passed with only minor occasional incidents. Every now and then, Diane would hear footsteps or smell cigar smoke, but that was the extent of it.

Jenny and Kelly were growing up fast. Jenny was already in her second year of college and Kelly was in her last year of high school. The subject of ghosts was never discussed; however, events still occurred that revealed the truth.

For example, on several occasions, objects would be missing, only to turn up later in strange locations. Diane was sure the ghost was responsible. Says Diane, "One time Kelly was hollering that she couldn't find her mascara, and she was having a fit. And I said [to the ghost], 'Okay, that's enough of it. It's getting on my nerves. Put the darn mascara back!' I had walked in the bedroom and looked for it and it was not on her dresser. After I said that, I walked back into her bedroom and there it was. I thought that was pretty funny."

The haunting continued. The activity was steady, but infrequent enough that the family was able to handle it and largely deny it. Then suddenly and without warning, the haunting erupted into an explosive frenzy of paranormal activity. Before long, the entire family became embroiled in a bizarre series of ghostly events.

It all began when they decided to convert the den into a bedroom for Jenny. As any ghost researcher will tell you, remodeling an old house can sometimes anger an otherwise peaceful ghost. In this case, they only redecorated the room and moved in Jenny's belongings.

For the first month, everything seemed fine. But there was one strange thing. The family dog refused to go into the room. Jenny tried everything, but he would not enter. She even dragged him in, but the dog cowered and whined the entire time.

Then another time, she was walking into her room when she distinctly heard her bed creak as if someone was laying on it. When she came in, however, nobody was there.

Jenny just dismissed the incidents. However, a few days later, she was lying in bed when the ghost appeared right in front of her. Says Jenny, "It [the door] opened and shut by itself, and it had a latch on it. The door opened and closed and I saw a dark area near the door. Definitely our family had ghosts, or a ghost in that house."

Jenny says that she watched the latch actually raise up by itself and the door would open and close, exactly as if someone was there. The apparition always appeared to be a huge dark shadow towering about seven feet in height.

Jenny remained calm, and at first told no one. She already knew about the ghost and didn't want to alarm the family. However, when the incident happened a second time, and then a third, she realized that she had to do something. She announced to the family that her den was haunted.

Dan was still skeptical, but Diane speculated that the ghost might be Mr. Miller, the previous resident. However, it didn't make any sense that the apparition was so tall. Kelly had no trouble believing her sister, because she too was starting to have experiences. Like the others, she told nobody at first. Says Kelly, "My phone, at four-thirty in the morning, just went 'ding!', like someone had picked it up and put it down. It did this the Sunday night before. The fact that the phone just kind of dings like that at the same time every night, I think that's kind of weird. It just does that in the middle of the night, and I totally completely wake up just at that little sound.

"I don't want to believe this house has a ghost in it, but sometimes I do...my sister felt that way. The den where her bedroom used to be – her bed would squeak all by itself all the time...she used to sleep in that room and she thinks it's totally haunted....That's where my other phone is, so if someone picked up the phone in that room and hung it up at the same time every Sunday night at four-thirty in the evening, it could do the same thing."

Kelly experienced other bizarre electromagnetic phenomena. The alarm on her clock radio began to go off in the middle of the night, even though it wasn't set for that time. This happened on several occasions, causing Kelly to become alternately terrified and annoyed.

The haunting of the Robinson household now including a huge range of activity including footsteps, odors, doors opening and closing, toilets flushing, strange crashing noises, objects disappearing, the phone dinging, the dog cowering in fear, the bed squeaking by itself and a seven-foot tall black apparition.

Around this time, Diane admitted that she had also begun to see apparitions, mostly out of her peripheral vision. "You know how when you're in the house, and you're in here alone, you might feel like something else was in here. You could almost think something moved between the living room door and the hallway. And you think, 'No, that's not my eyes.' Sort of like a streak of light. Weird."

Diane could no longer deny that her home had somehow become the epicenter for a series of inexplicable events, and that her entire family had become embroiled into an alarming state of affairs.

Dan was a scientist who worked on confidential government projects. He was a logical man and stubbornly refused to believe that a ghost was in their house. Having never had any paranormal experience, he assumed his family was overreacting to imaginary events.

Jenny and Kelly dealt with the issue by ignoring it. Nobody really knew what to do about the situation. So instead of confronting the spirit, the Robinsons continued to act as if nothing was wrong. It was the old adage of ignoring the elephant in the house. However, in this case, it was a ghost.

Meanwhile, Diane began having dreams of horrible tragedies that would come true the next day. For example, she dreamed of a bus accident in Mexico that killed several people. The next day it was on the news.

Diane couldn't understand why she was having these dreams, but she knew that they were somehow connected with the haunting.

All these events were beginning to wear down her will power. She felt like she was being slowly taken over by the ghost. She couldn't believe that Dan still remained skeptical.

Soon, however, events would occur that would leave everyone in the house stunned and totally convinced that there was indeed a ghost in the house, and a powerful one. In Kelly's bedroom, there is a large oak dresser that weighs nearly a hundred pounds. It comes to shoulder height and is solid and heavy. It takes at least two people to lift it, and this is when the drawers are empty. Kelly keeps her drawers packed full of clothes, books and other possessions. The dresser is located about two feet to the left of the door on the inside wall.

One day, Kelly was alone in the house, which was something she didn't like to do. She was in her bedroom and had walked out momentarily. When she returned a few minutes later, she reached out to open her door, but it wouldn't open. Something was holding it closed.

With chills running down her spine, Kelly forced open the door. To her shock, the heavy oak dresser had moved several feet across the floor, blocking the doorway. And there was nobody in the room. Says Kelly, "My dresser was all the way across the bedroom door, where I couldn't get back in. And I don't know how the hell that can happen. Who knows? I don't know."

As soon as Kelly realized what had happened, she fled the house without hesitation. She ran straight to her boyfriend's house across the street and spent the night with him.

Unfortunately, in these types of cases, the haunting can follow the witnesses and spread like an epidemic. When Kelly told her boyfriend what happened, he told her that he, his cousin, and his roommate had all noticed strange activity in their own house. Says Kelly, "He's also had weird things, like he thinks people are outside looking in. He gets all freaked out. He was telling me, and his roommate told me, that they come home and they didn't know who was in there, but they came home and their things were all moved around, like people were looking at the stuff they had in the house but never took them. That's happened a lot."

As Jenny was spending most of her time at the nearby college and both parents worked, Kelly was often left alone in the house. Rather than spend the night alone, she usually went over to her boyfriend's house. On these occasions, she would know that the house was totally empty. But when she looked across the street, the lights would be on in her room. Says Kelly, "We've had it where I'm over at his house and my room light is on, but I didn't have it on. And then I'll find out if my mom and dad were in there, but they'll have already gone to bed. He's like, 'Oh, there's somebody in your room.' He thinks it's funny. I don't."

Following the dresser incident, Kelly told her parents. Dan thought the whole idea was preposterous and refused to discuss it. Diane, however, could see the fear in her daughter's eyes and knew she was telling the truth. Says Diane, "Kelly went to go in her room to get her shoes or something, and she had the door closed, and the door would not open. So she shoved and here it was, the dresser had moved over in front of the door, and yet there was no earthquake or any rhyme or reason for this. So she told us about it and we were kind of, 'ha-ha,' you know."

At this point, the pressure was building towards the breaking point. While Dan clung to his skepticism like wreckage in a storm, an event was about to occur which would shatter any doubt that he had about the existence of a ghost. It was a perfect case of poetic justice. Having denied the possibility of a haunting for so long, Dan was about to come face-to-face with the impossible.

Diane and Dan were alone in the house. Diane was cleaning up when she found a pair of Kelly's shoes that had been left out. Grumbling at her daughter's messy housekeeping habits, she walked up the stairs and put the shoes in Kelly's room. She left, closing the door on her way out and walked back down the stairs. She then walked into the kitchen where, to her disbelief, she found another pair of Kelly's shoes. Exasperated and annoyed, she marched back upstairs, grabbed the door handle, and tried to open the door. To her surprise, the door wouldn't budge.

She called over her husband to help. Says Diane, "I try to open the door, and the door to her room will not open. So I say to Dan, 'There's something strange. The door is stuck.'

"So he comes and says, 'What do you mean the door is stuck?'

"'Well, there's something in front of the door.'

"'Well, how could that be? Nobody's in her room.'

"And I said, 'Well, something's there.' So we shoved and it was the dresser. And it was almost half-way across the door, which is a pretty heavy dresser to be shoved across the door like that. It's to the left of the door. There are two dressers and that one had moved clear over. And to move that clear over would take quite a force. And there was no one in her room, nobody in her room.

"It had moved, and I mean it was full of stuff. It was heavy. I could not move it. It was over the door. And how the heck it got over the door so that we couldn't open the door – it took Dan to open it – I'll never know. And that's happened twice."

The incident frightened Diane more than any other incident to date. Dan prefers not to discuss the incident, though he does admit that it happened.

Around that time, both Jenny and Kelly decided to move out. They both said it had little to do with the ghost, that they just wanted to live their own lives. Diane wasn't so sure, but in either case, she certainly understood. Both her daughters were grown up and had boyfriends and careers.

Shortly after her children moved out, another incident occurred. Diane was looking for something which she thought might be in Jenny's room. But when she opened it, she felt something blocking it. She called her husband, and together they heaved open the door. This time it was blocked by a large cardboard box filled with books, photographs, and other belongings.

The two of them looked at each other and didn't say a word. The subject was pretty much taboo.

Then came the day Diane was almost possessed. Her memory of the event is sketchy. All she remembers is that she was alone in the house. Slowly she became aware that she was not in total control of her actions. It was as if somebody had taken control of her body and was using it. She remembers slowly waking up and realizing that she was scrubbing the floors over and over again. She says that it felt like somebody was not so much forcing her to clean, as having had taken over her body and doing what they pleased. When Diane finally realized what was happening, she stood straight up and walked straight into her bedroom and began praying.

This was a procedure she had adopted following the dresser incident. Evidently it seemed to work, for following the near-possession, the haunting slowed down considerably. There were still small incidents, but they were few and far between.

Diane later learned that Mrs. Miller was an obsessive cleaner of her house and she wondered again if it was their spirits that were causing all the activity. At that point, she didn't really care. She was just happy that all the activity had finally stopped.

Maybe it was because the children had moved out. Maybe it was because the den was vacant. Maybe it was because Diane had prayed that the ghost would cease troubling them and find the way to where it belonged. In either case, the haunting was over.

One of the last incidents occurred in 1992. Says Diane, "We heard this big clash. Dan's grandmother had some paintings. One was hanging over the electronic organ in the living room. And we heard this big crash and looked all over. We couldn't see what happened, what it was. So a couple of days later we came home from work and I looked, and I said to Dan, 'Where is the painting over the organ? Where is Gran's painting?' And he said, 'Oh, my gosh, I don't know.'

"So we looked and the picture was down behind the organ. The nail was still up there on the wall and the picture was behind the organ. It would have had to lift up over this big nail. It would actually have to be lifted up to just crash down. There's no way it could have just come off unless the nail had come out of the wall. But the nail was still there."

Another more recent incident occurred in 1995. Diane and Dan were alone in their bedroom. Says Diane, "I woke up in the middle of the night and the flashlight was on over by Dan's bed. It's one of those little expensive flashlights. It comes in a little case and you have to really turn the top to make it go on. It just doesn't go on easily. And I said, 'Why do you have the light on?'

"He said, 'I don't know.' And the next morning he told me he was scared out of his wits because it went on by itself.

"And that wasn't the end of it. The next night, I was going to bed and the lights were out in the bedroom. When I looked, the flashlight was on, the same one. And I thought, 'Gee, why did he put that on?' And when he came back in I said, 'Why the heck did you put the flashlight on?' And he said, 'I didn't. I didn't put it on, Diane.'"

Kelly also reported that in her new apartment, she saw a black apparition run across the living room. And one time in the middle of the night her *Dust Devil* vacuum cleaner turned on by itself. Otherwise, she had no other experiences.

Diane is still not sure who the ghost was, but her main theory is that it was the Millers. Although the activity has pretty much ceased, Diane still occasionally feels an uncomfortable presence in the house.

She explains, "I have to admit if Dan goes camping I turn off all the lights on in the house. And if one light goes off, I'm out of here. I'm across the street to the neighbors. 'Hi, neighbors! One more person over here, you don't mind, do you?' I'm not a brave person. I'm not afraid of the house, but when Dan goes camping I don't like to be here."

# 24 — When Poltergeists Knock

On the outside, the Sorenson family (pseudonym) of Van Nuys, California appeared to be the traditional American family with a husband, wife, and three children. The husband worked full time, the wife stayed home and cared for the children, two boys and one girl. They lived in their house in the suburbs. Everything seemed perfect.

However, on the inside it was not perfect. The husband was abusive and suffered from alcoholism. Mrs. Sorenson finally made the decision to divorce him for the sake of her children. At the same time, her oldest son got into drugs and following numerous attempts to rehabilitate him, she was forced to kick him out of the house.

After years of raising her children and not working, Mrs. Sorenson was forced to hit the streets and find a way to feed her family. After much persistence, she finally landed a job at a large aerospace company. She started at the bottom but quickly worked her way up to the position of quality control inspector.

Her job definitely helped to pay the bills, but it also took time away from her children. Then one day in 1977, her youngest child, Mitchell, then thirteen years old, broke his leg. It was to mark the beginning of one of a long and involved haunting that ended in the near possession of Mitchell. It all began with strange knocking sounds.

Mitchell was ordered by his doctor to spend the entire summer in bed. He was diagnosed with a condition that left his bones weak and delicate. Needless to say, this was very frustrating for him. It was during this time that the strange knocking noises began.

Says Mitchell, "The first incident that I remember was back when I was thirteen, when I was recovering from having a broken leg. I was lying in my bed in the middle of the night and I kept hearing – at first it wasn't really a knocking; it sounded like footsteps in the attic, above the ceiling. And then all of a sudden, there was no noise. Then it sounded like there were footsteps in the hallway. Then that noise went away. And then that was when I heard the knocking for the first time.

"It didn't really sound like someone knocking on the door. It sounded like someone was knocking on the ceiling. I don't know how to describe the noise. It wasn't like pounding. It wasn't like someone was pounding on the door. It was more like someone was doing a normal knock, like someone knocking their knuckles on the table. And there were only three or four knocks, and it went away."

Mitchell was not scared by the knocking sounds, just curious. He wondered what was causing it, and why it was happening. But after several minutes, it went away and he fell back asleep.

In the days that followed, he continued to hear the knocking noises. It was as if some kind of door had been opened. Says Mitchell, "What was strange about it was that most of the time, the knocking occurred it was during that summer. And definitely at night, usually from nine o'clock on. It was never in the early evening."

Mitchell recovered from his injuries and returned to normal life. However, every summer after that, the strange knocking noises returned to his bedroom. "It happened almost every summer and as far as I know, no one else heard it. When I was asleep, it never woke me up. But when I was awake, just lying there at night, I would hear a knocking. And sometimes I would hear the knocking above my bedroom. Sometimes I heard it out in the living room or in the hallway. And one summer in particular, I don't know if it was loud, but it seemed like it just went on. It seemed like the knocking just kept going all night long."

As the knocking became louder and more frequent, Mitchell started to get frightened. The knocking was suddenly more brazen as if whoever or whatever was doing it was aware of his fear. Mitchell searched in vain for an explanation. "It's funny because there were times that I thought maybe my sister or Randy [his mother's boyfriend] or somebody was in the hallway. I'd open the doorway and no one else would be up. There would be no one in the doorway, and the sound would be gone. And I was sitting there, and I would feel like, 'What, am I going crazy? It must be the wind, right?' And I'd go back to bed and sit there and it would start up again. And I'd be thinking, 'Well, how can the wind make knocking noises in the attic?'"

Mitchell didn't want anyone to think he was insane, so he told nobody about what he was experiencing. Unknown to him, however, his sister Nancy had also begun having strange experiences.

Nancy's first experience occurred around the same time as the knocking noises and involved an apparition. She was walking in her front yard with her friend Cathy when they both heard an eerie hollow, fluttering noise.

Cathy was the first to see the ghost. She explains, "When we started walking back towards her house, it was kind of dark. And we heard this whistling behind us. And as we walked, the sound seemed to stay kind of even with us. It was kind of an inconsistent sound. It didn't really sound like it was coming from a person. It just seemed to be there. And we both got really scared, so we decided to start singing. I remember singing to try and keep ourselves focused, from being afraid and from being disturbed by whatever this thing was. When we turned the corner, there were lights. It was really dark during that whole period. And then we saw a man standing there, and it looked more like the silhouette of a man."

Nancy doesn't remember hearing any whistling noise, but she does remember hearing Cathy suddenly start singing. She wondered why her friend had suddenly burst out in song, it seemed so illogical. And then she saw why. "We're walking down the street on my side of street, and we notice this image in his [her neighbor's] driveway. It started up near the house and it started moving down the driveway. And as we got closer and closer to his house, it came closer and closer right down the driveway."

At this point, Nancy was confronted with a strange mystery. The figure she was seeing looked like her neighbor, an elderly man. And yet, not only was the figure ghostly, she sensed intuitively that the ghost was not her neighbor at all, but was trying to fool them. Says Nancy, "It was an image. It was actually like a ghostly image. It didn't seem solid. It was like an apparition of him. It looked like him, but it wasn't him. I wasn't paying much attention. Cathy noticed it before I did, and she started singing *I Am Henry The Eighth.*

"And when I saw what she saw, I started singing this song with her. This thing, it's like it moved sideways. As we were walking down the street, it was looking at us and moving sideways. It wasn't walking. It was sort of shuffling. I wasn't scared until we got kind of close to it."

Cathy was also convinced they were seeing a ghost. "He appeared not to be moving normally. Instead of walking like a normal person, he kind of walked sideways, from side to side. Almost like he was flat, sort of shuffling sideways, side to side. So that got us really scared. But we kept walking though. I think we kept singing too and just kept with where we were at as not to be distracted by what was going on around us.

"But we never got near this person enough to really see him. It was always like we stayed at quite a distance, and I can remember it being always a shadow of a figure, and just kind of staying off to the distance. When we got back we were very scared. We felt kind of distorted."

Nancy had never seen a ghost before, but she had no doubt she was seeing one now. "It wasn't transparent, and it didn't look solid, but it wasn't actually see-through. As we got closer to the driveway, it sort of turned to face us. And it sort of wobbled. It didn't stand still, and it didn't looked like it was actually standing on the ground. We just passed him and then once we got back down to my house, we turned around and looked at the driveway, and he wasn't there."

Within a few weeks of that time, Nancy was in her bedroom working on her college homework. Suddenly, the strange knocking noise which had plagued Mitchell for years returned. Only this time, there was another witness. Says Nancy, "One of the first times I noticed it was after we saw that thing in the driveway. First it was really subtle. There would be this creaking on the roof. Now, in my room there was no attic. It was just tongue-in-groove paneling, and the roof was right on top of it. So when there was something creaking on the roof, of course you always thought, 'Okay, there's a cat on the roof. The squirrels are playing. The wind's blowing.' It didn't really mean much because in that room there was no insulation; there was no attic.

"So at first I didn't pay any attention. I'd hear creaking on the roof, and then after a while, it would get heavier. A period of time goes by and the creaking becomes more and more obvious and more pronounced. As time went by, the creaking became more obvious. And it was less and less like creaking and more intentional, like creak-creak-creak-bang-bang-bang-BANG!"

Nancy became increasingly puzzled by the noise, but did her best to ignore it. She had begun to realize that it was probably something strange and she didn't want to give it any attention. To keep herself from getting too afraid, she simply ignored it.

And yet the knocking continued to get worse. Says Nancy, "It was almost always late at night when there was nobody awake in the house. And I'd be sitting in my room studying. And here would come this knocking on the roof. And for a long time I just kept saying, 'Okay.' I just kept putting it off. I didn't want to accept the fact that there was something hanging around bugging me.

"And then it must have realized that I wasn't accepting it. So it started moving down into the walls so that there could be no question that there was something there. I couldn't pass it off as, 'Oh, there's a squirrel running in my wall between my kitchen and the bedroom.'"

Nancy was now sure that their house was haunted, and yet, like Mitchell, she told nobody. She was sure the ghost was trying to scare her, and she was determined not to give in to its games. She would stay up late at night doing her homework and studying when the knocking would return. The more she ignored it, the louder, bolder, and more frequent it became.

Nancy, however, still refused to let it scare her. It became a strange game of cat and mouse, with her trying to ignore the ghost, and it doing its best to get her attention and frighten her. Says Nancy, "Sometimes it would knock right up the wall next to me. I decided that whatever it was, was fine. It could be there and do whatever as long as it didn't come in my room and actually bother me. I was being the typical human; I was afraid of what I didn't know and couldn't actually see. So I wasn't really that interested in finding out what it was.

"I used to hear it every night for a while. But it occurred to me that it was feeding off my fear. So I started ignoring it. Because as I became more scared, it became stronger and louder and more disturbing. And so at some point, it wasn't wise for me to be afraid. Because the more afraid I became, the louder and more rambunctious it became. So at one point, I actually told it that it should go and find what it was looking for somewhere else. I didn't want to feed its negativity. I didn't want to feed it with fear.

"But it never went away. It just kept hanging out. And I'd ignore it. And it would hang out, and I'd ignore it."

Nancy didn't know what else to do. She was hoping that, like a bully on the school playground, by ignoring the ghost it would eventually go away. And after she confronted it, the activity did seem to slow down slightly. The knocking would still occur periodically, but it was less and less.

Finally she decided to approach Mitchell and ask him. She asked him, "Do you ever hear noises on the roof?"

Mitchell said, "What, like squirrels?"

"No, not squirrels....well, it might the spirit of a dead Indian or something."

Mitchell replied, "Well I don't know." Mitchell didn't know what to say. As he later reported, "She was scaring the hell out of me to tell you the truth."

Then one evening Nancy was up late at night studying in her bedroom when the now familiar sound of knocking began again in earnest. She was ignoring it, but Mitchell walked in and heard it too.

He looked at her and said, "Do you hear that?"

"Yes," she replied, wondering what he was going to say.

"Well, what is it?"

Nancy replied, "I don't know. It's been hanging out in here for almost a year now, and I don't know what it is."

"Well, why don't you find out?" he asked.

Nancy just laughed and said, "Because I've never had enough gall. I don't have the courage to find out what it is, to tell you the truth."

Mitchell, however, was becoming intrigued. He was surprised and kind of glad that his sister had also heard the knockings. At least he wasn't crazy. He didn't tell her that he had been hearing the sound for years. He thought it was only him. Now it was bothering his sister too. What did it want?

Mitchell's reaction was the opposite of his sister's. He began to give the ghost more and more attention. It was around this time that he noticed the knocking sounds coming from more and more locations around the house. At times, he felt like the ghost was purposely trying to scare him or drive him crazy. Says Mitchell, "Sometimes I heard it in the bathroom. That is what was weird. It was never someone knocking on the doors or walls. It was always the floor or the ceiling. And I never caught anyone when all this was happening. I never caught anyone awake or anything. I was the only one. That's why I thought I was maybe going a little bananas or imagining it. But it happened so much that I thought, 'Well, there's got to be something to it.' I never really pursued it as far as going into the attic or anything."

Nancy didn't realize that her brother was also experiencing the knocking noises. They both assumed that the ghost had appeared only to them.

Mitchell's recent interest in the source of the activity, however, seemed to ignite the power of the poltergeist to a new level. Says Nancy, "It used to happen only in my room until he became curious about it and started saying, 'Well, what is it? What could it be?' So a couple of days later, he was taking a shower and it started knocking on the shower wall. It scared him."

By now the activity was building to a frenzy. However, it still stayed discreet, appearing only to Mitchell and Nancy and never to their mother or her boyfriend, both of whom knew nothing about the ghost.

Around this time, Nancy had a vivid and powerful dream about the rape and murder of a fellow classmate. Two days later, the dream came true.

Meanwhile, the knocking was coming more and more often, and Mitchell became torn between terror and fascination. He also began to sense a presence outside his bedroom door late at night. As he says, "There have been times when I felt someone was in the hallway, but when I opened the doorway, there never was. And that was always in the middle of the night too."

The haunting was now reaching its peak. Because Mitchell had given the ghost attention, it was now manifesting more strongly. It was a few weeks following the shower incident when Mitchell was physically attacked by the ghost, which then actually tried to possess him. Mitchell reports that this incident remains the single most terrifying event of his entire life.

It was late at night and everyone else was asleep in the house. Mitchell closed the door and crawled into bed. In the middle of the night, he was woken up by the familiar knocking noises. This time, however, there was something else – footsteps.

Says Mitchell, "Well, it was kind of weird. I heard footsteps up in the attic, like someone was walking around up in the attic. And then it sounded like the footsteps walked from the living room to above my bedroom. And then they disappeared. There was no more walking. But someone was tapping every ten or twenty seconds, and then there would be one or two knocks.

"This is the part that I really don't tell people about because it's kind of weird. People say, 'You might have a vivid imagination.' It like…progressed. Usually after that point, it would die off for the night. But it didn't this time. That's what was really weird. All of a sudden, I heard the tapping go from my bedroom ceiling to the ceiling over the hallway. And then it stopped. And then I swear I heard someone walking in my hallway. And I got up as fast as I could and I opened the door. There was no one there.

"I was trying to rationalize it, right? So I shut the door. And that's when I swear I heard someone knocking on the floor, right in front of the door, like tapping on the carpet. And that's when I just said, "I'm not going to answer the door this time. I'm going to stay in my bed.'

"And that's when I felt…I felt like someone was in the room. And at that point, I turned on the flashlight that I had – a little *Mag-lite* – and there was no one there. And I turned it off and laid back down, and I still felt like there was someone in the room.

"Then, at that point, it felt like someone literally stepped on my bed.

"At that point I didn't move. It was dark, but I could see that there was no one in the room. But it felt like someone was standing on the foot of my bed, at my feet, just standing there, standing on top of the bed.

"I just closed my eyes and didn't move. And the pressure being felt on my bed was pretty real. Not at first, but after that I did feel like someone had not really *stepped* on my legs, but had like *laid* themselves down across my legs. It never reached up to my face or anything, just on my legs."

By now Mitchell was absolutely terrified. He waited to see what would happen next. Says Mitchell, "I could move. It was easy to breathe and everything. It wasn't like they were pushing on my chest or arms. It just felt like someone was standing on my bed, and then it felt like someone laid down on my legs.

"I mean, I don't know if it was a person. When I had the feeling of someone stepping on my bed, I raised up my head only and I could literally see the bed bending. Now when they laid down on my legs, I didn't lift my head up. I didn't move. I just closed my eyes and listened. But before I did, I could plainly see there was no one in front of me. And the door was closed the whole time. No one opened and closed the door. I would have been able to hear it."

Mitchell lay there, and although he wasn't particularly religious, he began to pray fervently. Slowly the pressure lifted. Says Mitchell, "And at that point, I heard one or two knocks again, above my bedroom in the attic. And I still had this feeling of weight on my legs. And then slowly the weight lifted off my legs again and I could just feel it on the bed. And then that feeling went away completely. And that was it for the night. And that was really the strongest incident that I ever remember. Everything else was like walking or knocking."

After the ghost finally left, Mitchell lay in his bed literally shaking with fear. He had no idea what had just happened to him. As he says, "To tell you the truth, I was sweating. I was slightly sweating and I didn't know what to think. I figured, 'Well, I could say automatically it's a ghost. It's a poltergeist or whatever.' But I don't know.

"But I would swear there was something in that room that night. And I would swear that it was real. And I never told anybody about it because nowadays you could easily get branded as a crackpot, a crazy, or whatever. So I basically kept it to myself. I only told a few people."

One of the few people Mitchell told was his sister. Nancy clearly remembers the day he came and told her that she was right to ignore the ghost, that he should have left it alone.

Nancy verified everything Mitchell experienced. "One night he was lying in bed when he heard the knocking above him. And he decided he'd be brave and he'd do what I wouldn't do. So he said, 'Well, what are you?'

"And he said he felt this pressure come down on his body. He said he couldn't see or feel anything. He just felt all this weight on his body. So then he started saying, 'Oh, Jesus! What is this thing? Jesus, take this thing away! I believe in Jesus! I believe in Buddha! I believe in the Savior! Don't let this thing hurt me!'

"His mind just said, 'That's my hold on reality. That's what I have to rely on.' And he started calling on the forces of good, and the thing lifted off, and went away and never came back."

Following this apparent near-possession incident, the activity came to a near-complete halt. There were still a few scattered knockings here and there, but nothing near the intensity of the weeks before. Says Mitchell, "There were times after that that I heard noises. But never like that. It was like creaking. It was never walking or knocking….I don't live in my mom's house anymore. And ever since I moved into this apartment, I haven't had any instances like that. And I've never been in anyone else's house with that instance occurring. Only at my mom's house. And I never told my mom or Randy about it, because I know them. They'd say, 'What drugs were you doing that night?' It wasn't drugs…if people want to call me a crazy or a crackpot, I'll say, 'Okay, well that's your opinion.'"

I was able to talk to another witness who, upon visiting the house one evening, distinctly heard footsteps walking across the roof. He had been told about the ghost, but didn't believe it. He reports that the footsteps were loud enough to be obvious.

Fortunately, since Mitchell confronted the ghost, it has never been back. Both Mitchell and Nancy are puzzled as to the identity of the ghost. The house was brand new when they moved in and nobody had ever died in the house. The cause for the haunting seemed to be a mystery.

It seems, however, to be related to the incident when Mitchell broke his leg. This would fit the pattern of a frustrated adolescent generating poltergeist like activity.

Whatever the case, Nancy and Mitchell learned the hard way that, when spirits knock, you don't always want to answer. Sometimes you don't know who or what you are inviting in.

# 25 – The Haunted Apartments

Some hauntings are more intense than others. In this next case, two girlfriends in their early twenties decided to rent an apartment together. Little did they know that they were about to experience the most frightening four months of their lives.

The experience left them so traumatized that they were extremely hesitant to even discuss it, not only because the horrible ordeal brought up so many awful memories, but because they were terrified that the ghost might come back. They didn't want to do anything that would expose them to the experiences that they had just been through. I honestly had never seen two more frightened people. And after they told their story, I saw why. It turned out to be one of the most intense and harrowing hauntings I have ever investigated.

The ordeal began when Trudy Shay (not her real name) decided to move out of her parents' house and live on her own. She was in her early twenties, had a steady phone-sales' job, and just felt like it was time. She searched for an apartment and found an ad in the newspaper that caught her eye. There was an apartment in a good neighborhood of Van Nuys, California for only six hundred dollars. This was a very low price and just within her price range. She was excited and decided to check out the apartment.

To her delight, it was perfect. The building was newly-painted in bright cheery colors. The grounds were well maintained with flowers and nice green lawns. It was a cozy two story building and contained only twenty-five units. All of the apartments were spacious and Trudy was thrilled to discover that there was also a pool. It was just what she was looking for.

The manager was very nice and showed her the vacant unit, apartment fifteen. Trudy fell in love with it right away. She had her own protected parking space and there was a locked gate. It was very close to the theater where she was rehearsing a play. The residents of the building were mostly older people so she figured that there wouldn't be too much noise.

The apartment fulfilled every qualification she was looking for. It almost seemed destined, too good to be true. She didn't hesitate. She paid the manager first and last month's rent and a security deposit.

The apartment was already vacated so she moved all her things in that week. She felt great to be living on her own, working towards her career as an actress.

It was June of 1987. At first, Trudy was nervous about living on her own, but to her delight, everything went great. She was working, rehearsing in the play, and having a good time living on her own. Sure, money was tight, but she was doing well enough.

However, about six months after she moved in, Trudy had her first problems with the apartment. One of the tenants in the unit directly below her was making too much noise. It sounded to her like he was throwing a tennis ball against his ceiling in the middle of the night, sometimes for hours.

This awful thumping sound would wake her up at night, and she would be unable to get back to sleep. It had happened so many times, that Trudy was about complain to the manager. But then, to her delight, the man below her moved out. Finally, she thought, she'd be able to have a peaceful night's sleep.

She was wrong. Even though the apartment below her was empty, the strange sounds continued. And when Trudy complained to the manager, she found out that the man below her had moved out because he thought that *she* was the one who was making all the noise.

Trudy couldn't believe what she was hearing. As she says, "Things were happening, but I didn't connect it. Now I look back, I think, 'Oh, my God! That's what it was!' The guy had moved out below because he thought I was making a lot of noise. There was a constant noise, now that I connect back to then, and I thought he was throwing a tennis ball against the wall. It was going *de-DE-de…de-DE-de*…constantly, hitting the wall, the floor and something else. And it kept doing it, a constant beat with a ball. But I never noticed it then. It didn't connect because I didn't believe in that [ghosts]."

Even though strange knocking noises were keeping her up at night, Trudy still didn't connect them with ghosts. She assumed the building was settling, the water pipes were knocking…or it was something else. The sounds seemed so regular. But she didn't know what they could be so she tried to not think about it.

Around that time, however, she started to notice other strange things going on in the building. She had moved into the building hoping it would be quiet. However, besides the knocking, Trudy noticed that an unusual amount of arguing went on in the building. It seemed that somewhere in the building, somebody was always screaming and fighting. In fact, Trudy remembers that several people were actually evicted from their apartment because of the continuing tirades.

Trudy also noticed that there were an unusually large number of old people in the building. She knew when she moved in that some of the residents were old, but it seemed as if virtually every unit was inhabited by very old people. It felt like she had moved into a retirement home, and Trudy heard from her neighbor, Carol, that several people in the building had died recently. Death was not a rare occurrence. There was a constant parade of ambulances going to and from the building.

Trudy learned that an old lady had died in the apartment next to the one that was directly below hers, and that also a young infant had actually died in her apartment. She was shocked to hear that so many deaths had occurred in the building. It seemed macabre and it definitely bothered her. But she had already moved in, and it didn't seem like any reason to move out. She was definitely not the superstitious type.

Still, there were other strange things. Everybody in the building seemed shy and reserved, almost scared. Everybody's door was always closed and locked, and nobody seemed to want to make friends with their neighbors.

Trudy didn't think much of any of this. She still loved her apartment, except for one thing – she couldn't afford it. Her bills had begun to add up. She had no idea she would have so many expenses. After several months, Trudy knew she would have to either get a roommate or move back in with her parents.

The choice was obvious, but finding a roommate wouldn't be easy. Who could she stand to live with? Then she thought of her new friend, Karen Tyler (pseudonym.) Trudy had met Karen while rehearsing for the play she was in. Karen was also in the play. The two of them started talking and found they had a lot in common. It wasn't long before they were close friends. Then when Karen mentioned offhand that she was looking for an apartment, it seemed like destiny had delivered Karen to her. She offered to share the apartment.

Karen accepted the offer and moved in at once. It was just before Christmas. Almost immediately after she moved in, strange events began to occur. They were setting up all of Karen's things, but needed help with the stereo system. So they invited their friend Ivan to help. He had been there only a few minutes when something happened. He was hunched over the stereo, fiddling with the wires when he suddenly stood up, looked over towards the hallway and the bathroom. His face turned chalk-white, and he was obviously frightened. Karen and Trudy asked him what was wrong. Ivan looked at them with hesitation and then finally said that he was seeing a lemur in the hallway next to the bathroom.

"What's a lemur?" they chorused, looking towards the empty hallway. Ivan said he didn't know what they were, but he called them lemurs. They were little creatures that he saw only when there were ghosts around. They were not physically there, but Ivan said he could still see them.

Now Karen and Trudy began to look afraid. Ivan said simply, "Oh, don't worry about it." And he bent down and began fixing the stereo. But both Trudy and Karen could tell that he was trying to set it up as fast as he could without looking like he was rushing. And the minute he was done, Ivan excused himself and left the apartment.

Trudy and Karen didn't know what to think of his statement that there were lemurs or ghosts in their apartment. Trudy didn't say anything about the strange knocking noises because they had stopped shortly after Karen moved in. Besides, she had no reason to think they were related. And when Ivan mentioned ghosts, she just laughed it off.

Karen, on the other hand, seemed worried by Ivan's announcement. She hadn't told anybody, but she had started to see strange things out of the corner of her eye, dark shadows that would flit across the hallway, exactly where Ivan said he saw the lemurs. Karen suspected immediately that the apartment had a little ghost.

Then about a week later, they both witnessed something that left no doubt in their minds that their apartment was haunted. It was early evening and both of them were alone in the apartment.

Says Karen, "The first time I really noticed it, we were talking in the bedroom and I thought I saw – it looked like a woman was looking around the corner, but neither of us said anything to each other. I was kind of freaked out, and I looked at her, and she said, 'What?' And we both saw it, and then we acknowledged it. It was just a little old lady."

Karen says that seeing the old lady frightened her badly. She couldn't think about the incident without getting chills all over her body. The thought of ghosts made her very uncomfortable.

Trudy, the more skeptical of the two, was also badly frightened. As she says, "We both saw it, but we didn't say anything. Something was there."

Following the short conversation, they dropped the subject. Neither of them wanted to talk about ghosts or admit that their apartment was haunted. Their strategy to deal with their problem was simple – ignore it.

Shortly following this incident, Karen began to see more dark apparitions flitting down the hallway. And now she wasn't seeing them out of the corner of her eye; she could look directly at them. "I'd always see figures running by the bathroom. The bathroom was here, here's the corner, and the bedroom was here. And I'd always see black figures running past the bathroom. A black thing. I'd be watching TV and see them back over in the hallway. It looked like stick-figures running by, black stick-figures."

Trudy also saw the apparitions. A few times, they were in the living room or bedroom, and the shadowy figures would run in, float up towards the ceiling, where they hovered in the corner. "They were dark figures. You could actually see the shape of the head. And the main part we saw of them was from around the shoulders to the head, because they'd always be peeking. And if you saw them run, you'd see like a dark zoom! The bottom – you couldn't really see it much when it would run."

Karen had only been moved in for about two weeks when the apparitions became more and more brave. Says Trudy, "Every single night! Every single night, the heads...the heads and the shoulders mainly, every night darting across. I mean, every time. I never saw the whole body so much. All you saw was the darkest area, the head. That was the darkest area. This area was actually see-through. It was dark, but it was fast, really fast. It was never slow. The only time it was slow was when it was peeking."

By now Trudy and Karen had admitted to each other that the house was haunted. They had developed a routine following each incident. Each time there was an apparition, they would look at each other and cry out, "Did you see that?"

The apparitions appeared so often, that Trudy and Karen noticed patterns. If ever they started arguing, the figures would appear and dash bravely right next to them, or float up in a corner and stare down at them.

At this time, although they were scared, both Karen and Trudy felt that the figures were not harmful. Playful and curious perhaps, but not malicious.

They wondered who the ghosts were and why they had appeared so suddenly on a nightly basis. The only explanation that they could come up with was that the entire building was being remodeled, renovated and repaired, and this had somehow woken up the ghosts.

They were friendly with the manager of the building, so they asked her about the remodeling. They learned from the manager that several strange things had been discovered. The construction workers had found several closets on the basement floor that had been permanently sealed. They had to be torn out for the remodeling. When they were opened, the workers found several old scrolls of parchment with writing on them. They were recognized as Jewish mezuzahs. On them were prayers that were supposed to offer protection from evil spirits.

Karen and Trudy looked at each other with knowing shock. The manager saw their concern and told them there was something else. When the workers reached the actual earth underneath the building, they saw that it had been mysteriously worked up and turned over. All the workers were spooked because they couldn't understand how the soil could have been so torn up after the foundation of the building was already laid down.

As the remodeling continued, the haunting of apartment fifteen began to escalate. Trudy and Karen felt their entire belief systems collapse as bizarre events occurred with increasing rapidity. The events were so absurd and unbelievable, the two young women felt like they were walking around in shock half the time. Reality was no longer following its natural laws, and it seemed like anything could happen. They began to feel like the haunting was moving inside them, possessing them. Says Trudy, "We felt really different. We felt really, really different, like everything was unreal. Like we were in a higher state of consciousness. Everything you looked at was really, really weird."

Karen also felt like the haunting was overwhelming her senses and numbing her mind. She felt almost like some force was taking over them and that they were no longer completely themselves.

This feeling seemed to be verified when Karen went to visit her good friend Pam. She knocked on her door and Pam answered. But Pam looked at Karen as if she was a complete stranger. Says Karen, "I went to visit Pam. I went over to her house, and I'm knocking on the door and nobody's answering. And they were expecting me. Then I see her looking around the corner and she's looking at me really funny. And she still didn't answer the door! And I'm saying, 'Pam! What's going on?!'

"And finally she opened it. And she said it was really weird. She was looking at me and she didn't know who it was for a really long time. She said it didn't look like me."

Pam clearly remembers the experience and says that it was one of the more unusual events in her life. She had known Karen for years. They took dance classes together. But when Karen knocked on the door, all Pam could think was, "Who is this stranger at my door?" It took her a long time to recognize that it was actually Karen. And even stranger, there was no reason for it, no change in hairstyle, clothes or anything. It didn't seem to make sense.

At the same time, Trudy had a very similar experience that was equally upsetting. Several of the residents in the building owned dogs, and both Trudy and Karen noticed that the dogs in the building were also sensitive to the activity. Says Trudy, "The animals in the building were always seeing things."

Their neighbor had a dog and whenever it was in their apartment, it would stare at the closet as if something was in there. Trudy loved the dog and it loved her. Every day Trudy would pet the dog and it would respond with friendly licks and tail wags. One day, however, Trudy went to pet the dog and it didn't recognize her. It barked and growled as she got closer. Says Trudy, "It ran from me. It was really weird."

The incident upset Trudy badly. They decided it was time to take action. The first thing they did was ask their neighbor, Carol, who lived across the hall, if she had any strange experiences in the building. They expected her to tell them that they were both crazy. Instead Carol said, "Well, my apartment is haunted." She revealed that she'd be alone in her apartment when someone would tug her hair. She'd turn around and there would be nobody there.

At first it was only once in a while, but soon it started happening several times a week, and then several times a day. She rushed to the doctor, afraid that she might be having some kind of seizure or nerve-disorder. The doctor, however, gave her a clean bill of health.

Carol then said that she hesitated to mention the next thing because Trudy and Karen would think she was crazy. The two of them assured her that they had seen a few crazy things themselves. Carol then said that wherever she went, a tiny white moth would flutter around next to her. It would appear and disappear constantly all day long, even at work.

At first it was just the hair-pulling and the moth. Then one day Carol said that she was putting on her make-up and the moth was fluttering in front of her above the sink. Suddenly, she saw the apparition of an old man in the mirror. She whirled around in fear, but nothing was there.

Finally, she said that there were strange noises at night. Karen and Trudy were too stunned to ask what kind of noises. Not only was their apartment haunted, so was their neighbor's. They had come asking for help, and instead, Carol needed help as much as they did.

A few days later, Carol was not in her apartment, but both Trudy and Karen saw activity happening in her unit. Says Karen, "We saw the lights going on and off over there. We also saw the shadow of a man go through the door."

They were beginning to think the entire building was haunted. Their unit itself, was becoming more and more uncomfortable. A strange musty odor filled the entire area, and there were also cold spots. Says Trudy, "Yes, that was mainly in the hallway, that area where we saw most of the stuff. And the bedroom."

So far, the activity had been strong for only a two weeks, and they were hoping that it would slow down. Instead, the activity became stronger and began to manifest in a number of different ways.

One day when they turned on the faucets, instead of streaming downwards, the water sprayed out sideways. Says Trudy, "The water would shoot out like somebody stuck their hand underneath the faucet. It was just like somebody stuck their hand under the water. Any time we turned on the water, it was like when you put your hand against the faucet. And we'd say, 'What is wrong with this?' And you couldn't fix it. You know how you try to redo the screw-thing? There was nothing wrong with it."

They were able to duplicate the effect by pressing the palm of their hands against the opening of the faucet. It happened with both faucets and it would only occur sometimes, unpredictably. First they would work, then they wouldn't, then they would. Another thing that made no sense.

Around this time Trudy's sister, Patricia, came to visit and stay for a week. Trudy almost canceled the visit because Patricia was a superstitious person, easily frightened by the supernatural. But they decided that the chances were she could spend one night without anything happening.

That night, Trudy and Karen slept in the bedroom while Patricia slept on the pull-out couch in the living room.

In the middle of the night, they woke to hear Patricia screaming in stark terror. Says Trudy, "We never wanted to tell my sister because she's really sensitive to that kind of stuff, big-time. So we said, 'No, we're not going to let her know about it.' She was sleeping on the pull-out couch, and all of a sudden, she was screaming. And she was yelling, 'Get away from me! Get away from me!' She was screaming and yelling, 'Trudy!!!' She was yelling for me to run there. So I ran out there and she was just saying, 'Get it away! Get it! Get it away!'

"And I said, 'What?', you know, knowing.

"And she said, 'Something is in here. Something was coming at me. It was going to get me. It was someone. It's someone outside.' She thought it was this girl coming to get Karen. It was right by the bookshelf where she saw it."

Karen and Trudy comforted Patricia as best as they could. Afterwards they both just looked at each other, knowing what the other was thinking. Now they weren't the only witnesses. First there was Ivan, then Carol and now Patricia. The ghosts, they realized, were getting braver.

By this time, not one day went by where something unexplained didn't happen. The haunting seemed to be escalating and getting stronger on a daily basis.

Around this time, Trudy was taking an afternoon nap alone in the bedroom. Her bed was a giant king-sized old-fashioned wooden bed. It weighed well over a hundred pounds and took three men to move in. Patricia was down by the pool and Karen was out. Suddenly, Trudy woke up to the bed shaking.

This had happened several times already, but she assumed that it was the building shaking or a small earthquake. This time, however, it was obviously only the bed. Everything else in the room was still.

Says Trudy, "I was asleep in it. It constantly did it. It was always going de-de-de-de-de. And I woke up and it would stop. And then it would start to go and it would shake."

Trudy promptly canceled her nap and found something else to do until Patricia and Karen were back. She told them what happened. The three of them had no idea what to do.

It had been three months now, and the activity continued to increase. Patricia was washing her hair when someone tapped her shoulder. She whirled around and no one was there.

One particularly frightening incident happened when Karen was taking a shower. "I was taking a shower. I was getting ready for the play, and I really saw them [the apparitions] going by. I went into the shower and I saw silver coming around me. I was kind of scared, it looked like dripping silver, dripping down the shower walls."

Karen didn't know what to think of the incident, but it felt to her like the ghost was trying to drive her crazy.

After a week, Patricia left. While she was there, the apparitions had started to appear less and less. But after she left, they came back in earnest. Also, the bed started shaking every night. They had been sharing the bed since it was so large. Every night when they went to bed, the bed would shake.

Says Karen, "It shook like an earthquake."

Says Trudy, "The bed was shaking, it wasn't even back and forth. It was like a really hard shake the minute we'd try to go to sleep. Now this is why we barely got any sleep, because of that. Any time we'd try to go to sleep, the bed would go thud-thud-thud-thud. We were told to tell it to stop. Our friends said, 'Tell it to stop.'

"So we'd go, 'Get the f–k out of here!' We'd look, because they would always be peeking. And then it would start. They'd peek and start. Peek and start. We'd say, 'Get the f–k out of here!' They'd stop. And then they would go again. Sometimes they would be in the room, but they would always be there when it happened."

The ghosts appeared nightly, shaking the bed and disturbing their sleep. Says Trudy, "They would want us to get up at night and play. That's what it was like. Any time we wanted to go to sleep, they'd shake the bed and wake us up. I'd say, 'Get the f–k out of here!' We'd even scream it. We'd just scream, 'GET OUT OF HERE!!!' I'd be crying, I was so afraid."

Not surprisingly, they both quickly became exhausted. Tempers often flared, and they started to get in violent arguing matches. Each time they argued, the apparitions would appear, as if they were enjoying it.

Karen is as certain as Trudy that the bed would shake by itself. As she says, "The bed started shaking more often, and then the bed started shaking every night. *Every* night. Big-time, every night. I'm thinking about it. Sometimes they [the ghosts] would be in the room. Sometimes they wouldn't. Sometimes the bed would shake, and I'd always look. I would think it was Trudy because she would move. And she would say, 'Whoa, did you do that?'

"And I'd say, 'Yeah, yeah.' I would be in a space where, when that tipping thing would happen at night, I'd always feel that it was more a feeling of her than me. I'd be there with it, but I felt a little outside of it somehow. It was more her than me. So I'd be really strong about it. And it was weird that I wasn't afraid because usually I was. But more, it was a feeling like it was messing with us. I'd say, 'This is my space! This is my space! You can't be here! This is my space right now! Leave us alone!'"

The two girls finally decided that they had to seek outside help. Their friends' advice of shouting at the ghosts only seemed to make it worse. They tried reasoning, pleading, ordering, cursing, praying – nothing seemed to get rid of the ghosts. The bed continued to shake and the apparitions kept flitting about the apartment.

Trudy was living on the edge of terror and Karen was putting up a false façade of strength. They considered moving out, but neither could afford it. They began asking everyone they knew for advice. While most were supportive, few knew what to do. A couple were skeptical of the activity. Says Karen, "We had friends come over to visit. The living room door was open at the time. And we were talking. She didn't really believe us. We were saying it was by the bathroom, and this and that. And she said, 'Oh, yeah, right!' All of a sudden, the light popped, and I saw it go out the front door, and she saw it go into the room.

"It actually popped. It was like a shoot of light that went out the front door, and a shoot of light that went down the hallway and into the bedroom. I was terrified. At that point I thought, 'How am I ever going to be able to sleep in this house?'

"Trudy got right up there and fixed it. Me, I couldn't. I was going, 'When am I going to grow up?'"

Needless to say, their skeptical friend was now convinced. Says Trudy, "She was joking. She went and stood in the shower, and she was laughing. Karen was explaining the silver stuff, and she went, 'Yeah!' So she went in the shower and she felt a little weird. That's all. She said she felt a little weird. So she came out of the shower. But then the light bulb popped, and all of us were just sitting there on the couch with the door open. It was really bright. And the light didn't even reach to the door. That's really weird because you saw it come from the door. I saw the light pop and go out the door. She thought it came in from the door. The light completely shot across, like a lightning bolt from the light.

"We were told to confront the situation. So I got up on this thing. I had to go right in the area, which was really scary for me. So I got up and changed the light bulb right away."

Karen's friend Pam gave them a sacred Tibetan snow-leopard mask, which they hoped might chase away evil spirits. Unfortunately, the bed continued to shake.

One friend told them that sea-salt is supposed to stop hauntings. Another recommended burning white candles. Karen and Trudy sat down and discussed the matter. They were supposed to put the candles and salt in the haunted area, but their entire unit was permeated with activity. There wasn't one single area where something hadn't happened.

They weren't sure if it would work, but they were desperate. They pooled their money and bought the supplies.

At this point, the situation became almost humorous if not for the fact that Trudy and Karen were both so serious. They opened the bags of sea-salt and at first they sprinkled it in neat little lines along the hallway. They then poured a huge pile next to the wall-heater where so many of the apparitions had been seen. They sprinkled some in the bathroom, then in the corners of the living room and the bedroom. Then they poured it liberally all around their bed until it was surrounded by a thick perimeter of salt. Still they had pounds of extra salt, so they poured it all through the apartment. When they were finished, the floors, counters, shelves and all surfaces were white with salt.

Then they got out the candles and set them all over the counters, on top of the heater, in the bedroom, bathroom, living room and kitchen. After a few minutes, they had more than two dozen white candles set up.

They then lit all the candles and prayed for the haunting to stop. Slowly the candles burned down to nubs and went out. They went to bed, hopeful that the ghosts had left.

No sooner were they almost asleep when the bed started shaking as hard as ever. The only result from the whole ritual was to make the apartment even more musty-smelling.

The next morning they cleaned up the mess. Before long new phenomena began to occur. Trudy's bike which she kept in the kitchen, never seemed to be in the same place she left it. She didn't tell Karen about it because she didn't want to alarm her.

Then one night while they were watching TV, the apparitions became particularly bold, flitting back and forth across the hallway over and over. Trudy and Karen had learned by now that it was best not to give the ghosts too much attention. So they tried to ignore the ghosts and keep watching the TV.

Then suddenly a terrible racket started up in the kitchen. Karen explains, "It was a really heavy-duty night. They were all over here. We were getting exhausted by it. That night we were in the living room watching TV. We were watching a video tape in the front room, and it sounded like they [the ghosts] were working in the kitchen. And I'm going, 'Oh, my God!' So that was kind of strange thing. It sounded like chopping, and moving pans and shutting cupboards."

This time Trudy was too frightened to confront the situation, so Karen got up as quietly as she could and peeked around the corner into the kitchen. The noise stopped instantly. Karen saw nothing out of order.

And so the activity continued. Trudy had noticed that the bike kept changing positions, but she kept this knowledge from Karen so as not to scare her. However, a few days later, Trudy had to go out and leave Karen alone.

Says Karen, "This is what happened. Trudy was over at a friend's house down the way. She was going over, and at this point, I knew what was going on. I was pretty fed up. I said, 'Okay, fine. If you're going over there, I'm leaving the door open.' Because I didn't like to be there alone.

"I thought, 'My God, what am I going to do? Everything around here in this apartment is falling apart.' I said, 'I don't want you to forget, I'm right here by the door.'

"And she called [on the phone] and she said, 'How are you doing?'

"I said, 'Oh, I'm okay.' And I take a look, and the bike that's usually in the kitchen is right in the living room. And I said, 'Trudy! Trudy! Did you move the bike?'"

Trudy hesitated to answer, which just made Karen more frightened. Says Trudy, "I said, 'Yes,' because I knew what was happening with the bike. The bike was moving from one area to another all the time. We didn't actually see it go across, but it would be in one area and the next. And we weren't doing it to each other. Why would we do that? No way, because I never moved my bike from one area to another. I never rode it during that time."

Around this time, Karen woke up one night from a horrifying but realistic dream. She was in a room with three other people when a man pulled out a gun and threatened to kill them all. He waved the gun around, as if he was possessed, and then began shooting. He shot and killed everyone in the room, and then killed himself. In the dream, Karen ran out of the room screaming.

She woke up in a cold sweat, thankful that it was only a dream. However, that day on the news, Karen saw her dream come to life. A few blocks away from their apartment, a man shot and killed his family, and then himself. Trudy and Karen were both horrified. It was exactly like her dream. It was as if she had actually been there.

At this point, Karen and Trudy were near the end of their ropes. They were constantly nervous and exhausted. Neither of them were getting enough sleep. Neither was comfortable in the apartment and they tried not to let the other out of their sight. Thankfully, their lease was about to run out, and they began scanning the newspapers for a different apartment. They had no intentions of staying there one day longer than necessary.

Trudy had spent a total of twelve months in the apartment and Karen only six. Ever since Karen had moved in, however, the haunting had become progressively worse. Now it was only two weeks before the lease ran out, and things were worse than ever.

Four days later, the haunting reached its peak. It was late at night, and both Karen and Trudy were getting ready for bed. They crept into bed and turned out the lights.

Then Trudy suddenly started praying with an intensity she had never felt before. She prayed to God and started saying the Lord's Prayer over and over. She felt the haunting coming to a peak, and she was more afraid than she had ever been. Says Trudy, "We were starting to move. We were looking for a place. There was a musty smell. Musty, dark, cold. But I guess you're in a state where you're not afraid anymore. I was praying all the time.

"I was just totally tired. We were both really tired, vulnerable. I'm crying all the time because it was happening. [I would say] 'Leave us alone!' Crying, pleading, oh!

"I'm saying the Lord's Prayer over and over again. 'Our Father who art in Heaven...,' over and over and over. And I was just clenching, and just laying there. I was *so* afraid that night.

"I kept saying to Karen, 'I don't want it to happen tonight. I don't want it to. I can't anymore. I can't deal with it anymore.'

"I was so afraid. All of a sudden, the bed started going really hard. But what happened...oh, I'm getting all scared now...the bed started shaking. And Karen felt this also. The bed was shaking.

"And I felt a pressure. I could not breathe, right here in my chest. It's like I broke away. Karen said it looked like I had been pushed back. But I couldn't breath. I could not breathe. I opened my mouth, and I can't even repeat the noise. And it was hard and fast that it came out of me. The only way I can explain it is that a vacuum was stuck in my mouth and sucked the air out of me so fast. Everything went. I mean, I couldn't even get up!

"And I was just crying. I said, 'Oh, my God!' crying and crying. Karen was looking at me like she didn't even want to touch me. And I was trying to breathe."

Karen was lying right next to Trudy on the night of the incident. She was becoming annoyed by Trudy's constant praying. Then the bed started shaking violently, the apparitions appeared, and Karen saw her roommate pinned down by an invisible force.

Says Karen, "That night was really, really weird. We were looking for a place, and we were ready. There was a musty smell. It was yucky. You'd walk in there and you felt like...dark, cold.

"This is what happened, now. We go into the room and we turn out the light. The candle is lit. Anyway, Trudy's really getting into it. And I'm thinking, 'Oh, come on, Trudy!' I'm kind of irritated. I'm starting to go to sleep and she's praying big time. I could feel it.

"And I'm next to her at this point. I remember she was laying like this [pressed down on the bed.] She was kind of stiff, kind of like it was holding her down. It was like she couldn't get up. She looked like she was trying to get up, but she couldn't. Then she sat up really fast. She couldn't go back to sleep."

Trudy says that not only was something holding her down and choking her, it had moved *inside* her. Says Trudy, "It went through me. The pressure here [on solar plexus], I could not breathe. And the minute my mouth went open, she [the ghost] was out. I was hoping she was out.

"When it went through me, that hurt me so bad. Not just breathing hurt – pain – like crushing."

Trudy was numb from the shock of being nearly possessed. She had felt the ghost actually move through her body. But now she had another problem, the ghost seemed to be inside her. She couldn't get its image out of her mind.

Says Trudy, "I couldn't go back to sleep. Any time I closed my eyes, I would see a lady. She was little – very little, very fragile. The outfit was like a vest from the sixties, and colorful. This was a colored thing I saw, it was not black and white. She was old though. Her hair was greasy, stringy, with gray and black in it.

"All I remember was the mouth. The mouth wasn't like a big grin, but it was nice and sweet. And her head was tilted. Very sweet, not threatening at all. It was almost – to me – like an introduction, because I was afraid and so curious of who these people are, and why they are bothering us. I don't want them to do it anymore. It was hurting us.

"That's the night that I closed my eyes and it went through me that I saw her. And I told Karen, 'I can't sleep. I'm seeing this lady.' And I explained what she looked like. And I said, 'She's not hurting me, but she's there.' She was there, and she wouldn't go away. Finally I did go to sleep, and then I never saw her again. That was the last time. But now I know exactly what she looks like. Exactly."

That night was the last straw. When morning came they discussed moving out into a hotel for the remainder of their lease. The decision wasn't difficult. They decided to move out that day and not spend one more night in the cursed apartment.

They packed up in a frenzy of activity, throwing everything they owned haphazardly into boxes and bags. By the end of the afternoon they were finished. All the hard work had left them famished, so they chose to treat themselves to a dinner at Café 50s, a quaint little fast-food joint on Van Nuys Boulevard only a few miles from their apartment.

As they sat down in the café, they felt the thrill of finally being free of the ghost. Never would they have to spend another night in that hellish apartment.

Unknown to either of them, however, poltergeists sometimes have the habit of following witnesses. Trudy and Karen were about to find this out the hard way.

They sat together in a little booth. It was during the dinner rush and the restaurant was crowded. As they sat at the table waiting for their food, they both felt the table give a sudden lurch. At first neither of them thought anything of it. But seconds later, it started to shake.

Says Trudy, "It was packed. The place was packed. First we were sitting there, and he brought us our menus and the water. And you know how you sit there with your elbows on the table looking at the menu? All of a sudden, I felt movement on the table. And I looked at Karen and I said, 'Quit kicking the table!'

"And she said, 'I'm not kicking the table.'

"It was just a really quick thing. We thought, 'Oh, it's nothing. It's the people over on the other side kicking the wall, and it's hitting our table.' Taking it logically. We were totally doing that.

"Then what? Both of us were leaning our elbows on the table. The table, and everything on the table was clanking together. The stuff on it mainly. Our elbows were on it. And just our table. We looked. Everything was going ch-ch-ch-ch! Things were clanking together. I started crying. I was crying. Things were clanking together. The silverware was going ching-ching-ching-ching!"

The table was anchored to the wall by a single metal pole; it should have been immovable. Karen couldn't believe it, but the ghost had actually followed them into the restaurant! Says Karen, "We sat down at our little table, and she felt it shake first. Then we ordered our food. We were relaxing, and we were feeling pretty good. He brings us our food, hamburgers, puts them down. We were ready to eat. We were exhausted. And both of us picked them up. And the ice was moving. You could hear it hitting the sides of the glasses. I mean, the table was just going.

"I turned completely white. The waiter came over. He wants to know what's wrong. Trudy says that he doesn't really. I say, 'Yeah, right!'"

While Karen was turning increasingly pale, Trudy had called over the waiter to complain. She didn't know what to say, but she felt like she had to do something. Says Trudy, "There were a lot of people in there. We're looking around, but no one is seeing this. No one is looking at it. It stopped. We called the waiter. I said, 'Have you ever had any complaints about this table?'

"And he said, joking, 'Yeah, there's a troll coming up through the pole.' Karen was all scared and I'm crying. So he calls the manager over and she…I felt like punching the bitch; I'm sorry but she was. She said, 'Oh, it's an earthquake.'

"And I said, 'Oh, just our table? Not our seats, nothing? Just the table and it's an earthquake? Yeah, uh-huh!'

"And then the guy said, 'Well, maybe it's the people over there.' Just like we thought. So Karen gets up and she goes over and looks. It's two old people, like they're going to kick the thing."

At that point, the waiter started to believe them. Says Karen, "He started believing us a little bit. He told us about an experience he had."

Says Trudy, "He kind of believed us, but not really. Kind of like, 'Oh? Well, I've got a story too.'"

At this point, they both lost their appetite and got up to pay the bill. That's when the ghost struck again, and this time the waiter became a witness. Says Trudy, "So I'm paying the bill and Karen's standing back by the gumball machine. The gumball machine's just sitting there next to a jukebox. And I'm paying the bill. And Karen screams, 'Trudy!!!'

"I turn around and look. And the gumball machine is going ch-ch-ch-ch, really fast, right next to her. And we grabbed the waiter who did not believe us really. He looked and he turned whiter than white. The gumball machine was just going. It was shaking like the table was. And he freaked out. He *freaked* out. The three of us saw that shaking. It was right next to her. I was crying."

Karen saw the gumball machine move first. It was an old fashioned design on single pole with a round metal base. Karen was standing right next to it when it began to move. Says Karen, 'I said, 'Trudy, come here!!!' It had little green ones in it, and they were going back and forth. I'm trying to get Trudy to look and the waiter to see it. I would say a good ten seconds. It scared me."

The two young ladies paid their bill and exited the restaurant in a hurry. They drove away and went straight to a hotel. To their intense relief, they spent a peaceful night.

They returned to their apartment early the next morning, packed up all their boxes and moved out. They found another apartment nearby. It was more expensive, but hopefully it wouldn't be haunted.

As they set up their new place, it was understood that there would be no talk of ghosts. The subject was taboo. They had decided that everything would be normal, no matter what.

In the first few weeks, both Trudy and Karen did notice small unexplained events, an object moving, a strange noise, a light turned on by itself. But these were few and far between. They learned to totally ignore them.

To their delight, the haunting seemed over. But just in case, they decided to move again. They found a better apartment and completed the move. After the second move, the paranormal events came to a complete stop. The ghosts had finally left them alone.

Both of them were ecstatic. The experience had left them badly trauma-tized. Both agree that it was the most frightened that they have ever been. Says Karen, "It got to a point. We tried to play like it didn't though, that it wasn't scary. But then it would, oh boy!"

Says Trudy, "I'm getting the chills now. I mean, you get *scared*. But you're in a weird state. You don't know. You think you're making this up. We didn't tell anybody for the longest time. We thought, 'Are we making this up?'"

For Trudy, the scariest part of the ordeal was the night of her near-posses-sion. For Karen, however, it was when their skeptical friend had come over and taunted the ghost into a manifestation. Says Karen, "The scariest thing was when the light bulb popped. That really bothered me. And the first time I saw it peek around the corner. That was really yucky to me. It was weird when it went through her, but the weirdest thing for me was the feeling of the thing, like I don't know how I'll ever be here by myself. But when that light bulb popped, it was such a shock, a sudden light."

Later they heard from their friend Carol across the hall. She moved out only a few months after them. Carol told Trudy that after she and Karen had moved out of apartment fifteen, another lady moved in. And on a few occa-sions when the resident went out, Carol noticed the lights in the apartment turning on and off and the curtains fluttering, even though the windows were closed.

So it would seem that the haunting of the Van Nuys apartments contin-ues. Right in the middle of a densely populated suburb.

Before writing this chapter, I again visited the apartments to see what they looked like. The building was situated between two similar-looking apart-ments. It looked very modern with its white stucco walls and maroon-colored wood framing the windows and doors. There was an iron security fence and an intercom. The lawns were green and lush with lots of pretty yellow flowers. It certainly didn't look like the type of place you would find a ghost.

But I didn't stop there. I found the phone number of the manager of the building and called her up. I gave her a short summary of what happened in apartment fifteen and asked her if she had any comment.

To my surprise, the manager was thankful to hear from me. I was pre-pared to be politely excused. Instead, she reported that she knew about apart-ment fifteen, and also said that several other residents in different units had reported similar activity. Furthermore, the new tenant of apartment fifteen also complained about unusual events.

Says the manager, "Exactly. The woman who lives there now still experi-ences it. We've had a lot here. One we had was in a different apartment than the two girls rented. It was across the building actually, but on the second floor. And the girl there said that there was a moth – there was weird things that it was doing.

"Another one, the girl who moved in there now, she said that she felt somebody was watching her from the bedroom door…but she hasn't really said that much because everyone's probably going to think she's crazy if she keeps talking about it. And I personally had one where I walked into the living room. I walked in there and I felt somebody watching me. And I ran back into my bedroom because it frightened me so much. But I've never had that feeling since. That's the only time I've ever had that."

I asked the manager if she knew the history of apartment fifteen. She revealed a dark story. "What happened with apartment fifteen was an older man and an older woman were living there. And the man died, and the woman became friendly with the man downstairs who was a young man. And they were just friends I guess, but they became very friendly. But the older man never rested. And that's who they say the ghost is, because sometimes he feels angry. The girl who's in there now says it's like he's angry."

Several months later, I checked in on Trudy and Karen. They were no longer living together. It seemed that the ghost was back, and it was now centering around Karen. She continued to hear footsteps and feel strange cold spots. Then one day she was alone in her apartment when a large black apparition pinned her to the floor for the period of an hour. She refused to give a formal interview and wouldn't give any other details.

Trudy, thankfully, has experienced no further activity.

# 26 – The Wildwood Poltergeist

One of the most extreme haunting cases I have ever investigated occurred in a small house in the suburb of San Carlos, California. The haunting began in 1975 when the Wright family moved into their home on Wildwood Street. Although the house was seventy years old, it was in remarkably good condition.

At the time, the Wright family consisted of only two members, Mrs. Wright and her infant son, Whitney. When they first moved into the house, everything appeared to be normal.

However as Whitney grew up, things began to change. He reports that from a very early age, he experienced strange events. He doesn't remember exactly when they started.

The earliest events that he can remember, however, were always connected to his imaginary friend. Like many young children, Whitney had a pretend playmate. Whitney reports that he spent many hours with his pretend friend. He always knew that he was just pretending, and yet things happened that sometimes made him wonder.

Doors would open and close by themselves. Lights would turn on and off. As he grew up, he had long stopped pretending to have an imaginary friend, and yet, strange things continued to happen.

It was around age eleven that Whitney decided that his house was haunted. As his mom was a single parent and Whitney was an only child, he was often left alone in the house after school.

It was then that things began to occur. Says Whitney, "Ever since I was a little kid, little things would happen. Like I'd go around the house and shut all the doors, and my mom would come home from work and the doors would be open. Little things like that.

"When I was a little kid, I would get weird vibes, and I'd feel like somebody was watching me. So I'd grab a knife out of the cabinet, run through the whole house, look in all the closets and stuff, because I'd think that someone like the Bogey Man was here. And every time, there would be nothing there.

"And I would always hear sounds and stuff. I don't really remember, it was a long time ago. But I'd hear whispers, like wisps, not really saying anything in particular, but I'd hear things. So I always had the thought in my head that there may have been a ghost or something in here."

Whitney had no dramatic face-to-face encounters when he was a child, but little things like doors opening and closing pestered him constantly. He searched for an explanation. Thinking back, the first events involved his imaginary friend.

Growing up alone had left him somewhat isolated. He had to invent games to play and things to do. At the same time, his overworked mother didn't have enough time for him. This set up the volatile situation of a frustrated adolescent.

When he was little, he would sit with his imaginary friend and pretend they were having conversations and doing things together. He knew that none of it was real, that he was just pretending. However, occasionally things would happen that made him think again. Says Whitney, "When I was a little kid, I thought I had little experiences. I used to pretty much think there was a ghost. I used to play tricks and I would always pretend that I had a friend there with me. And it was weird, my mom would come and yell at me, and I would wish, 'Damn, I wish she would just slip and fall!' And she would slip and fall."

The first time this happened, Whitney marveled at the coincidence. Did he cause that to happen? It didn't seem possible. But when it happened again and again, he was forced to reconsider.

"One time I was pissed because she had grounded me, done all this stuff to me. I had some crayons I was drawing and she broke my crayons. Well she was putting up this thing; on our back porch we have this overhang. And it had like fiberglass material on it. And I'm thinking, 'Damn, I just would it would slice her head off or something!'

"And sure enough, she sliced her hand really bad. It was weird. Stuff that I would think, that I would want to happen in my mind, would happen. That's how I started to realize something was up.

"When you're a little kid, you live in a fantasy make-believe world, so you're not really scared by these things. It's natural. It's like, 'Wow! Cool!'"

As Whitney grew up, little paranormal events occurred on a regular basis that left him convinced he had a ghost in the house. His friends remember that he was always talking about his ghost. When Whitney was a teenager, his friend Paul Delgado moved into a room in the garage. It was shortly after Paul moved in that the ghost began to haunt the house in earnest.

Where before the ghost appeared infrequently, now things began to happen more often. And different types of phenomenon began to occur.

The first manifestation was objects moving by themselves or disappearing. In fact, this became the new preferred manifestation. The ghost would constantly take Whitney's and Paul's possessions. As usual, the two boys would blame each other and an argument would ensue. It was only later that they realized that the ghost was causing the problem.

Says Whitney, "It started getting bad when my friend, Paul moved in. He was living in the loft, and it would play little things against us, try and get us in fights. It would do little things, like I'd be missing something out of my room. It had this tendency. I would lose stuff, like my guitar tuner.

"The tuner is an electric cordless tuner that I tune my guitar with. Paul plays guitar too, and he would sometimes borrow it. One day I was tuning my guitar and the phone rang. So I went, and I was on the phone for ten, twenty minutes, came back, and my guitar tuner was gone. I was really pissed, yelling at Paul. And I couldn't find it.

"It was really weird. I looked everywhere in my room. I could not find it. Then we went back up into the loft, looked everywhere, and I couldn't find it. And Paul kept on saying he's been up there the whole time, and it was not up there. Finally I got to the point where I said, 'Forget it!'

"I searched every part of the house from one square foot to another. I went through the whole house and could not find it anywhere. I went through my mom's closet, underneath all her clothes, all her drawers, cupboards, everything.

"So finally we got to the loft, and we looked up in the loft again. I had looked everywhere except for these boxes, because my mom had these boxes from when we moved here, with old china. They were boxed up. They'd been boxed up since 1975. So I started looking for it in there, and sure enough, I found the tuner. It was wrapped in papers, in a wad of papers at the bottom of this box of china that had tape on it since 1975!

"I told my mom and asked her, 'Hey, have you been in this box lately?' She said, 'No.' It was buried up in the loft, and the tape was old masking tape. You can tell when masking tape gets old; it turns yellow and gets kind of crunchy. I wasn't even thinking about it. I was more in a bad mood. I was just tearing apart the boxes, looking, not really thinking about what I was doing. And then, all of a sudden I found it. It kind of blew me away."

The ghost had finally hit upon a method to get attention. After this incident, numerous valuable personal objects began to disappear or be mysteriously misplaced. Says Whitney, "I've had money disappear. Constantly, things are moving in my room, even to this day. But it's weird. If you let it get to you, that's when it gets stronger. If you don't pay any attention to it, and don't give it any energy, nothing really happens."

One of Whitney's and Paul's favorite pastimes was to get together and play guitar. They formed a small band, and played every chance they could get. Interestingly, the ghost seemed to hate them. During these jamming sessions, strong bursts of paranormal activity would manifest in various ways.

Says Whitney, "Another thing it hated was when Paul and I had a band. When we practiced here and played music, it would throw a temper tantrum. The house would be totally clean; my mom would keep the house clean. And then we'd play.

"Then we'd come out. The toaster and the can-opener have these covers – they'd be pulled off. And the cupboards in the kitchen would be open. Stuff would be on the floor. Not necessarily every time were the cupboards opened, but one time I can remember that. It would throw a temper tantrum when we would play."

Whitney had grown up with the ghost, and although it had never been so active, he was already familiar with the idea of strange events happening around the house. On the other hand, his friend Paul had never encountered such things as ghosts. He had never thought much about them and didn't really believe in them. So when unexplained things began to happen to him, he had the tendency to ignore them or explain them away.

It wasn't until the ghost began to steal personal objects and cause fights between him and his best friend that Paul realized Whitney was right, there was a ghost. Says Paul, "There were definitely unexplained presences that we were experiencing there. I really didn't know how to explain it. I was very doubtful of things. But there were just some things that happened that were very unexplainable. So many different things went on for a period of time.

"I can definitely say I have a belief in lost objects. Things that you know you've set somewhere, you come back, and they're not there. And you just know they were there. That kind of thing.

"It definitely seemed to mess with our heads. It seemed like sometimes the thing, in certain rooms, would get us very angry. And we'd end up being very agitated. And other times we would be just scared. Other times it definitely messed with your head. But you are just mainly in a state of denial, saying, 'This isn't happening. I'm just tripping out!'"

Another way the ghost manifested was through unexplained sounds. Most houses produce odd creaking sounds as they settle. The Wright household, however, seemed unusually creaky.

Whitney explains, "You know you houses, when they settle, they crack? We just had an earthquake up here, and my house was creaking pretty bad from it. But you would hear it tweak the house. It sounded like…you know how you wring out a cloth? It would ring out the house. The whole house would go, *creak*!!! You would hear it, and it would go through the whole house. It sort of shuddered. It sounded like it was tweaked, like it was creaking through the whole house."

Now that Paul knew about the ghost, he understood all the previous unexplained events. But now he had another problem, the ghost was still here. Paul didn't like the idea of living with a ghost. The whole idea scared him.

Several months after he had moved in, he experienced one of the scariest events of his life. It was evening and he was alone in his room, resting quietly. Says Paul, "I used to sleep up in the attic there. There's this little stepladder that goes up into the attic where I would sleep. It was above the garage, and all the doors were closed. And I remember I once experienced what sounded like somebody. I thought Whitney was messing with me and that he was walking up the stairs, because I could distinctly here the creaking boards. It was distinctly someone walking up the stairs. By the time it got up to where

I thought it was, I jumped up and looked around and there was nobody there.

"That was quite bizarre. They were all pretty weird, but probably the scariest one was when the thing sounded like it was coming up into my room."

The incident left Paul shaking with fear. There was no more denying that the house was haunted. He told Whitney what happened.

Paul suggested that they get a Ouija board and try to contact the ghost. At this point, he didn't realize that giving the ghost attention only made it more powerful. He only wanted to find out more information that would help them understand why the ghost was bothering them so much. He was also curious as to who the ghost was.

Whitney already had his theories. As he says, "The Jehovah Witnesses next door had a kid drown in their pool, a seven-year-old kid named Joey. And this was like our little nickname, calling this ghost Joey."

Whitney told Paul that he had no idea if the ghost really was Joey. It was just a theory. Paul wanted to find out the truth.

As Whitney says, "I had this girlfriend, and all this time Paul and I said, 'Wow, maybe we can communicate with it.' We got this Ouija board with a pendulum. It had a wire going down to a weight. You swing it and it swings over whatever it wants to say.

"The pendulum on the Ouija board, we would swing it back and forth, and it would stop in one area. It was fighting gravity to stop there. It stopped, paused a couple of seconds, and then it started swinging again. We asked another question. It would pause and stop swinging for a couple of seconds, then it would start swinging again.

"My girlfriend and Paul's girlfriend were all playing around with it, asking all these stupid questions. Actually I think it was telling them what they wanted to hear. They were having a good time doing it. I was saying, 'What the f–k is this? I don't want that shit.'

"They just kept on playing. My girlfriend was telling me what was happening, and I said, 'F–k that shit! Take it away! Don't even mess with that anymore!' She had her elbow on the table, holding the pendulum. I got pissed. I yelled at her. I said, 'Don't even f–k with that shit anymore or I'm going to throw you out!!!'

"And sure enough, right in the middle of the wire, it broke. It didn't jerk her hand around. It just went *tink!* and the weight hit the table. We were all, 'Whoa! Trippy!' We looked at it and it just broke right in the middle. You know how when you bend a wire back and forth, it finally breaks? You can see where the metal turns a little bit whitish? Well this was a clean break.

"But on the Ouija board, we were messing around with it, and my girlfriend got out of it how old it was, supposedly seven years old. And its name, Joey. And I think the ghost was playing on the fact that we had a kid who died in the pool next door, saying, 'Oh yeah, I'm this one.' Because it had an evil mind.

"That's the name we got out of it, and seven years [old.] I don't know how old the kid was that died in the pool next door. So we all friendly called it Joey."

Although Whitney doesn't believe that the ghost's name is really Joey, or that it's even a little kid, he calls it Joey anyway. He thought the Ouija board incident was all a waste of time.

Paul agrees. As he says, "It was like a fishing line, like a little two pound test with a little lead weight on the bottom of it. And you would hold it over a little board, and you would ask these questions, trying to communicate. And she was moving it around, and she was asking these questions. Don't ask me how, but all of a sudden the little test just snapped and fell. There's just no way to explain it. It was a perfectly good piece of string, and she wasn't pulling on it or anything. It just broke."

Although Whitney was not happy about living with a ghost, it did have certain advantages. For example, Joey was an interesting conversation subject. Whitney told all his friends about the ghost and talked about it constantly.

Most of his friends already believed in the ghost because they had seen it themselves. Around this time, Joey became so active that paranormal events occurred on a near daily basis. Whitney began to notice another pattern.

Whenever somebody came over to visit, *something* would happen. It was as if Joey delighted in scaring the guests and embarrassing Whitney. This happened so many times, that Joey became a well-known ghost in the neighborhood.

Whitney first noticed that the ghost would perform for guests when his teen-age friends would come over. He would warn them about the ghost. If anybody was too skeptical, Whitney learned that something strange was very likely to happen.

If Whitney declined to mention the ghost, then usually nothing would happen regardless of the visitors' beliefs concerning ghosts. But if he brought up the ghost and somebody announced their skepticism, the ghost would explode into activity.

Whitney was actually able to predict paranormal events using this method, and could in fact cause them to happen. He felt bad for scaring some of his guests, but on the other hand, he wanted to be believed.

Says Whitney, "All my friends come over and they don't believe it. And [then] it totally makes itself apparent to them. That happened a hundred times to all different friends of mine. They'd get doubt in their mind, and it would happen."

One by one, Whitney's friends had a rude initiation to his ghost. It became something of a joke.

One particularly memorable incident happened to his best friend. Says Whitney, "There was another friend that it did something to. He's like my brother; he's the closest friend I got. I still talk to him to this day. And when he comes over, he asks, 'Have you heard from Joey lately?'

"But we were sitting in the front room talking about it, and he's all, 'Man, you and Paul are freaked. This is bullshit!'

"This was one time when my house was trashed, and I'm saying, 'Look at this!'

"He said, 'Man, it looked like that when I came in.'

"I said, 'Bullshit! I swear to God!'

"He said, 'Man, don't! That's full of crap!'

"He was tweaking out. I'm thinking, 'Whatever…' But he was leaving, and we were going out the front door. And right then, we heard a *slam!* We had this overhang over my front door to keep the rain off the porch. And we heard a *slam!* up there. I'm thinking, 'What?! What is it? A cat or something?' I didn't know. I was freaked out.

"We both climbed up around the edges and looked up, and there was nothing there. It was quite a loud slam. It sounded like someone jumped up there with all their might.

"It was right when we were talking about it, and he said he was thinking in his head, 'This is bullshit!' He told me afterward that he thinks he triggered it because he said it was bull. He doesn't believe in that crap. And that's what happened."

Another similar incident happened to Whitney's friend, Dan Diaz.

Says Whitney, "Dan, I remember he heard something. And he ran outside and there was nothing there. I don't remember specifically what happened, but yes, it's true – it happened to all my friends."

Dan Diaz has known Whitney for more than twenty years. When they were kids, he remembered that Whitney insisted his house was haunted. Despite Whitney's obvious seriousness, Dan just couldn't bring himself to believe in the ghost. His reasoning was simple: ghosts aren't real.

For some reason, the ghost would not show itself to Dan. So although others insisted the ghost was real, Dan remained skeptical. Says Dan, "I've known Whitney since we were in the fourth grade. And he told me there was a ghost in his house. I didn't really believe him at first. He told me that it was a friend of his, and as he got older, the ghost always stayed its age. And I guess when they were friends, they were the same age.

"It materialized one time, and it was a kid. But I guess the thing would mess with him, play tricks on him, do things to him. And he always knew. And his mother knew too.

"He never told me anyone died there, but I think they knew who he was. And he could follow it, from the coldness. They usually knew where it was.

"I guess he materialized one time at the foot of his bed, when he was younger. He said it was a little boy, and he said it was in ragged clothes. He would always talk about it, and I never knew if I should believe him or not. But as we got older, he was always talking about it."

When Joey finally decided to introduce himself to Dan, it was not a pleasant introduction.

Dan recalls the incident in vivid detail as it left a lasting impression on him: "One time, we were in the attic, part of his house. It's in the garage, this loft area. We were hanging out up there, and we heard it. It came and it hit the roof right where we were. It knew right where we were. Just *bam!!!* Really loud. It wasn't a rock. And there were footsteps too, but there was no one there. It wasn't like anyone had been there.

"It was damn loud. It scared us all. He was like, 'Yep, that's him.' I can't remember his name, but he would call him by name."

By this time, Whitney was extremely sensitive to the ghost. He could actually follow it through the house. Says Dan, "He took me in the house and we walked around in all the rooms. And he's all, 'This is where he is.' I couldn't feel it, but he said he could."

As interesting as the ghost was, Whitney wanted to stop it. He had no idea what to do. His friends knew even less. He even asked a Native American Elder who told him only that he had a bad spirit in the house. Says Whitney, "He didn't really want to come into my house. He said they felt a presence and didn't talk too much more about it."

No matter where he turned, nobody seemed to be able to help. No matter what he did, paranormal events occurred on a regular basis. Says Whitney, "For years, every single night, at various times through the whole night, from little experiences to big ones, like I told you – it was heavy duty. To this day, about ten years are full of them. There are hundreds of them.

"When people say they don't believe, I'd like to bring them to my house on a heavy day. I would. They would be quite scared. Because the thing with this ghost – I haven't done it in a long time, but if I really think about it, and dwell and dwell, I could bring it back. It's very easy. If I really wanted to freak someone out, I could do it, I'm sure, just by bringing him into this house.

"At other times it plays little games. And at other times I have brought people here, and wanted to, but wasn't really serious about it I guess. And it has done stuff. But it's just weird games it plays.

"As far as anyone saying they don't believe in that stuff, I'd laugh at them. I'd say, 'Okay, on a heavy-duty week, spend a night in my house with no one there.' If they can have a conclusion or an explanation for everything that happened, I'll give them whatever I have. I'll give them my car.

"Sometimes I tell people about this, and they laugh at me and don't believe me. It really burns me up. It's like, 'What!? You guys are weak-minded!'"

While paying attention to the ghost definitely increased the ghost activity, the only effective method to slow it down was to ignore it. Says Whitney, "Ignore it and realizing that it was there and there's not very much you can do about it. The more attention you pay to it, the stronger it gets. When you try to ignore it, you pretend it's not there, it gets bored with little antics or whatever."

While ignoring the activity slowed it down, it didn't make it stop. The ghost continued to find creative ways to make itself known. Without failure, it seemed to know exactly what to do to cause an argument. Says Whitney, "The little games he plays are evil. Like when I had my friend that you interviewed, Paul. We would get into a minor little fight. And then it would be a bloody brawl. It would really agitate your feelings, like hiding little things, playing little games like that, which I think Paul did it or whatever."

Whitney reports that the ghost would even terrorize his animals. They had two cats and a dog. One of the cats seemed particularly sensitive to the presence of the ghost. Says Whitney, "One of my cats – I noticed a long time ago – when it was really strong he would get chased around the house. And he would want to get out of the house badly at times, when the presence would get really strong. It would start doing more mischievous things to me and Paul, and the cat would want to take off. It would definitely want to leave."

Whitney reports that the ghost seemed to actually follow the cat. "The cat would be chased around the house. He'd get in one corner, and then all of a sudden he would freak out and run to another side or part of the house."

The ghost also manifested with odors. Says Paul, "There was a time when certain rooms in Whitney's house – it definitely wasn't the smell of garbage. It was like a dead smell. We've smelled that before. I remember there were definitely horrible odors sometimes, and they weren't just normal odors like dirty socks or food or something."

Whitney says that one evening, he realized he could actually feel the presence of the ghost as a distinct cold spot in the room. In fact, the cold spot was so defined, he could tell exactly where it was. He was able to follow it around the house, though more often, it seemed to be following him.

Paul didn't doubt Whitney's assertion that he could physically feel the ghost. He too had noticed this phenomenon. Says Paul, "We would get cold flashes and you would know it was there. There was no denying it. We both experienced the same thing. We were standing near the bottom of the stairs there, Whitney and I. We were just standing there and we felt this coldness, this being or whatever just nudge us and walk right past us. It was really strange."

The two of them became fascinated by their ability to perceive the location of the ghost, and they decided to try an experiment. Once they found out where it was, they would step into the cold spot and try to feel the energy.

To their surprise, it almost felt like the presence would move *inside* them. Says Whitney, "We had been going on for a couple of weeks where you would get these rushes, like a head-rush [vertigo.] It would start in your back and tingle, and then it would go up to your head, and you would feel all your hair stand up. It's like when you're in a warm room and you get a breeze of cool air. You just feel tingly for a second. You're like, 'Whoa!' Like when you're in a hot-house and you run outside, and it's cold and you get that feeling. It's kind of like that.

"We had been playing with these rushes from time to time. And this one night we had gone in one room, and then we would wait there and you would feel it. You could honestly feel a presence fill up the room. It was really weird. You would get the rush, and instantly the room would feel cold.

"And we were going from room to room in the whole house doing that, because we were playing with it.

"This one time we ran into the kitchen and Paul said, 'Wait! Check this out!' Because it was following us from room to room. We could totally feel it. I mean, two of us were there. It was real.

"So Paul lit up this cigarette, just to see where the smoke was going. The kitchen was warm at the time, and the cigarette smoke was going off into another part of the house, I guess from a draft or something. And then the room got colder. It was late at night, and you could tell the cigarette smoke was going into the living room.

"Then all of a sudden, it stopped. And it started going straight up. It was really weird because at first we thought, 'Wow, we just came in. We are causing the wind drafts.' But we had caused the wind drafts going the other way. It came in there and the smoke was going straight up. And we both got a rush and felt really weird. We felt that cold feeling.

"We just played with it like that, time to time. And it seemed like my room was the most – I guess you could say possessed or whatever, because that's where the extreme things happened."

Whitney knew that they shouldn't be playing around with the ghost, but it was a lesson he had to learn the hard way. "I've always believed in God and been towards trying to be a good person. So I really didn't want to pay much attention to it, because it kind of scared me. And it was definitely evil to say the least. I didn't want to play with it. It's like something taboo. You don't really want to mess around with it, which you shouldn't actually."

Paul also learned the hard way that you don't want to play around with Joey. He recalled the night where they were able to feel the ghost's presence and step into the cold spots. Says Paul, "I remember we would walk into rooms in the house, and every room that we were in seemed to get really cold. We would leave the room, and we would go to another room. And then all of a sudden, it would get cold. And we thought, 'Hey, this is weird.'

"So for an experiment, I lit a cigarette. There was no draft in the house. All the windows were shut and there were no fans or heaters on. And whatever room we walked in, the cigarette smoke would seem to drink into whatever room we went to. And we would stay in the room for a while, then we would back into the next room, and the smoke would drift back into the room that we were in. It was really bizarre."

Whitney did not like playing with the ghost and knew that it was mistake. Paul, however, was becoming increasingly intrigued. He found the feeling of actually sensing the ghost to be a unique and thrilling sensation. Like Paul, he could actually feel the presence of the ghost.

The evening of the cigarette smoke experiment, they both retired to their separate rooms. Both of them had just got into bed when a piercingly loud screeching, grinding sound reverberated through the house. Both of them describe the sound in the same way. Says Whitney, "We were just getting ready to go to sleep when, all of a sudden we heard this weird sound. You know how an old-fashioned skateboard or skates have those steel wheels. It sounded like that, going down the street. But it was actually so loud and heavy it sounded like a car. This was really weird. It sounded like a car driving down the street with no tires. This was *really* weird. We were just getting ready to go to sleep and this sound came into our house.

"I heard it pass by the front door and go down the street. So I looked out my window instantly. I was all, 'What the f–k?' I couldn't believe it, so I looked outside. Nothing. [It was] totally normal.

"But it was weird. It sounded like a car driving down the street with no tires on the rims – just this grinding, squeaking, crunching sound. When things happen like this, you are constantly trying to figure out what made it happen. So I instantly picked out a car in my mind."

While Whitney was staring out his bedroom window at the front street, trying to locate the source of the sound, Paul was in his room in the loft. He heard the sound and thought that someone was pounding on the roof. As he says, "The most bizarre sound we heard was what sounded like an old metal skateboard with old metal wheels, screeching down the road. It sounded like it was going over the roof. We went out. We both heard it. He was clear on the other end of the house and I was in the attic. And we both heard it and couldn't figure it out. We looked in the sky. We looked around. We couldn't see it anywhere, but we heard this sound going down the street. It was weird. It was bizarre."

Paul dashed out of the loft in the attic and knocked on Whitney's bedroom door.

Says Whitney, "I was really tripping out on this. You could almost feel like something was really antsy. All of a sudden, I heard a knock on the door to my room. I'm all, 'What?!' I grabbed a baseball bat. I was all freaked out.

"I opened the door and it was Paul. He was scared. I mean, he looked like a ghost, he was white. He said, 'What are you doing messing around with me like that?' He thought I did the sound because he's up in the loft and there are no windows or anything.

"But to say the least, Paul was at my door, all scared. And he's yelling at me, thinking that I was playing with him. He said he heard the sound, and then for about three seconds, it sounded like it was raining on the roof of the loft. Where his bed was, you could reach up and touch the roof. He said it sounded like it was raining, but he said it was a lot louder, a lot harder than rain – like it was rocks on the roof or something.

"So he thought I was making some crazy sound and throwing rocks on the roof, playing with his head. He thought I just wanted to freak him out, to do that. So he says, 'Let me sleep in here.' That's true. That's what happened.

"I said, 'Hey, Paul. I promise to God I wouldn't do something that mean to you.' You know, torment him. That's something you don't really want to play with. I mean, that's something I wouldn't do."

Once again, Joey had tried to cause an argument. Although they were able to prevent a fight, the night had been particularly unnerving and both of them were still frightened.

Paul insisted on sleeping in Whitney's room, so they set up a bedroll at the foot of his bed and prepared to go to sleep. However, as soon as they lay down, they both felt the presence of the ghost very strongly.

Little did they know, but the haunting was about to come to a climax as Joey launched a full-out attack on the unsuspecting witnesses.

It all began when Paul started playing with the ghost again. Whitney tried to stop him, but it was too late. The experience occurred in 1983, but both remember it vividly.

Says Whitney, "I set up a bed so he could sleep on the ground. We were talking about it, freaked out. Nothing really happened. It was totally mellow. So then we decided to go to sleep. So he's laying there thinking, 'Man, that was trippy!' I mean, you get that small little bit of tinkling, like a rush, when it comes into the room. And he said, 'Did you feel that?! Did you feel that?!'

"I said, 'Yeah, that was trippy, huh?' And then it would go away. And we kept on getting them in series of three or four at a time. Then it would be quiet for a couple of minutes, and then they would start getting really big – I mean, heavy-duty.

"Paul was all, 'Wow! That's intense! Wow!' It started getting really bad, and he started saying, 'Wow! This isn't bad. Maybe it doesn't want to hurt me.'

"I said, 'Shut up, Paul! Just go to sleep! Forget about all that stuff!'

"And he started to say, 'No, no, I like it. It feels good.' He kept on saying that.

"I said, 'No! Come on!' I was laying on my bed. He was laying at the foot of my bed crossways. This incident is probably the heaviest thing that ever happened. I'll never forget it.

"He was all, 'No, no, I like it. I like it. This feels good. Come on! Come on! I want more! I want more!' He kept saying that. It was weird. He kept on saying, 'Wow! Wow! Did you feel that?'

"I was saying, 'Paul, come on!' And he was right in the middle of this big rush. To say the least, it stuck my hair straight out.

"I heard him. He was all, 'Wow! Wow! This is great!' And then, all of a sudden, it sounded like something grabbed his throat, like it made him start talking really squeaky. It was really weird. It was like someone squeezed his throat, and he kept on talking. He didn't go, 'Aaahhh!' and start screaming like someone was grabbing him. If something grabbed his neck, he'd be freaking out, especially if he couldn't see it. He didn't.

"It sounded like something grabbed his vocal cords and stretched them so he talked really squeaky. You couldn't really make out what he was saying. It was really weird. He wasn't stressed or anything, but he just kept on mumbling. My personal opinion, it sounded like some other crazy language or something.

"He kept on mumbling. I was laying there stupid, thinking, 'What? I don't understand this?' I didn't really believe it at first. I was all, 'What the f–k is up? What is happening?!'

"It was weird. I tried to sit up in my bed and it felt like gravity was pulling me down. It slammed me back in my bed. I sat up for one second, and it slammed me back in my bed. It was like I had five, six-hundred pounds sitting on my chest. But it wasn't really holding me at one point [on my body.] When something holds you down, you can feel it on your shoulders or your arms or whatever. It was like through my whole body. I couldn't even lift a toe. I was pinned there. I could not f–king move!

"I was struggling, screaming, because I heard Paul. He was starting to get squeakier and squeakier.

"It was really weird. It took what seemed like hours, but it was only a matter of minutes – I rolled off the bed. I hit the ground and I crawled. It was still playing with me, but it was like it lost its grip or something.

"I went right over to Paul, and I touched him. I still have scars. But I touched him. I had a crucifix on my neck. My neighbors used to be Jehovah Witnesses and they gave it to me a long time ago. So I put it to his chest. At the same time, he grabbed my back. I still have scars from it. I mean, it was a sharp pain. I mean, *it* grabbed me.

"It just kept on mumbling, mumbling in that squeaky voice. And as I held it there, I was thinking in my head, 'God, please help me!' And his squeakiness went back to crying, and he was sitting there crying. From him grabbing me, he started hugging me, crying, just totally shaking. He was really tripped out.

"To say the least, I was quite freaked out. I told him straight out, I was going to kick him out of the house if he ever plays like that again. And he honestly didn't realize what he was doing.

"My personal experiences from what I've talked to people with ghosts, it was trying to possess him in a way, get inside his body. To say the least, it almost did. It was quite scary. I still remember it vividly. That was probably the heaviest thing that happened. I mean, you would have to be there to experience it. It scared the shit out of me."

The two of them learned a tough lesson. When dealing with some ghosts, you can't be too careful.

Paul himself has only sketchy memories of the incident. Although he remembers sensing the ghost and feeling it enter into his body, his memory ends there. Says Paul, "I remember we felt this presence in the room, and we felt this energy. And I let it come into me. As I was doing so, I seemed to be overwhelmed by it. I remember being pinned to the floor…but I wasn't thinking or anything. I just remember I couldn't get up, and it was very strange."

Paul's next memory was of Whitney pulling him back into consciousness and being very upset and afraid.

Both of them vowed never to play with the ghost again.

Unfortunately, by this time, it was too late. The haunting was now at its most powerful. A few months following the near-possession incident, Whitney experienced an event that was equally terrifying. For the first time, Joey manifested in full-color.

It happened at the worst possible time. Whitney had just broken up with his girlfriend, and he was confused and upset. He lay in bed thinking dark thoughts. The ghost evidently couldn't resist the opportunity.

Says Whitney, "[Have I] seen it? One time. This is really weird. I had just broken up. I had this girlfriend I was really in love with, and she totally screwed me over. This was when Paul was living at my house. It got to a point, he was scared to even come home for a while. He says to this day he won't live in this house.

"But to say the least, I was really upset. It was really mellow. We hadn't any disturbances in the last couple of months. And then all of a sudden, I felt really weak. I was hurt. I felt bad. And I came home.

"We have this light in the front room that's always lit up. It lights up the front room and you can see through the drapes. It was like the drapes were pulled back with a face looking at me. It was like you could see it, but when you really start focusing on it and really looking at it, you can't see it anymore.

"It was really weird. I looked and looked. Even after that, I'm constantly thinking, 'Oh, maybe it was the cat.' Trying to constantly to find an explanation behind all this. I looked, and the drapes were pulled back. I went into the house, and I was all, 'What the hell?' I was kind of upset and pissed, but kind of scared at the same time.

"So I got into the house, looked at the curtains, and the curtains have been pulled back. Usually you would think wind, or the heater or something like that. But it was way up high. It was up like towards the top of the curtain, they were tucked.

"And I was just thinking, 'Damn, that's weird. Whatever.' I blew it off, so this is kind of foggy. I don't remember about this because it was kind of scary. But to say the least, that night I was really scared, weak.

"So I got in my bed. I laid down. I started trying to go to sleep. It was like I dozed off for a while. Then I got cold chills. I was kind of dozing off and I got a cold chill. I woke up and it *stunk!* My room reeked. I almost puked! I mean, I gagged when I woke up. You get a bunch of meat, and you throw it in the garbage can for about a half year, six months. It smelled gross. It smelled like rotten flesh, that's what I think. It was crude. My room stunk. It was cold. It was weird.

"I sat up in my bed. I had this chair my grandma gave me a long time ago. It was in the corner of my room. I saw this silhouette of a person, a small young person sitting there. I could tell the head moved. It looked at me, and it was weird.

"I woke up because it was stinking. It stunk! I looked, and I saw that. I was to the point, shit happened that was so heavy, like the thing with Paul, that this didn't really phase me too much. I just said, 'Oh, shit! What the f–k?' I laid back down, pulled the covers over my head and tried to go back to sleep, although I couldn't.

"It was weird. I felt it. I can't say that I heard it or anything. But I felt it right next to my bed all night. I mean, right there next to my head, like it just got out of the chair and looked right about six inches from my face. I wasn't one to go, 'Oh, wow, I'm going to look.' I just said, 'F–k it! I don't want any part of this!' I just laid beneath my covers, and then I woke up.

"That's about the best I can say that I saw it, a figure. Because it was so real that I probably could have reached out and touched it. It quite tripped me out, to say the least. It was after that thing with Paul happened. I was blown away after that. It was like, that happened, what could be worse?"

Shortly following the appearance of the apparition, the activity began to slow down and taper off. Every now and then, odd events still occurred, but nowhere with the intensity of before. There were a few odd creaks, a few missing objects, but that's about it.

Today, Whitney knows the ghost is still around, and that he could probably re-activate the haunting quite easily. But he refuses to do so. He learned the hard way. He knows that Joey's only intentions are to cause fear, and Whitney won't play that game. His invisible playmate is no longer welcome.

And although Joey is still around, Whitney has learned how to control the situation. He has adopted an attitude of casual boredom towards the ghost, and this has quieted it down almost completely. For several years now, only isolated events have occurred, usually involving missing objects. Says Whitney, "So much stuff has happened, little things. The last experience was just things in my room being lost, and not being able to find them. Not a major experience or anything. It's just constantly something. Like I have asthma. He has this tendency to hide my inhaler in my room. I can't find it. It's buried in the back of the closet when I hadn't even been by that closet in so long. Just little things, hiding stuff. It does that to me a lot.

"Like money. If I don't pay much attention where I put my money down when I go to sleep, it's not there in the morning. And I've never gotten that back, and no one even went into my room.

"It's to a point, it doesn't even faze me anymore. I'm kind of bored with it now. I don't really want to say that because I'm sure…I'm sure it's in here right now listening, because I'm in the house that's haunted. But like I said, it's been really mellow lately in the last couple of years.

"But it doesn't really faze me. I let it do what it wants. If it's not material, it inhabits this place too. If it's a ghost, and what they say about ghosts, it's been here a hell of a lot longer than I have."

Whitney was at first reluctant to even given an interview about his experiences because that would be giving the ghost attention. It turns out he was right. Immediately after the interview, the ghost came back. In a follow-up interview, he told me what happened. Says Whitney "Last time you interviewed me, I guess the presence in my house wasn't too happy because he took a checkbook. I was just getting ready to go downtown and do some shopping. He took my checkbook for about a week and decided to give it back to me about a week later, after we had searched the entire house, every inch of the house. He gave it back to me. He left it right in the middle of the kitchen, right underneath the kitchen table. And we had checked everywhere, in every part of the house."

I apologized to him for provoking the ghost, but he told me not to worry about it as it wasn't the first time, and wouldn't be the last. Whitney doesn't know why his house his haunted. Nobody ever died in the house. He is confident that the ghost is not the little boy, Joey, who died across the street. He feels that the mischievous and even malicious behavior of the ghost reveals its truly evil nature.

Another explanation is that of the poltergeist. It could be that Whitney has some mediumistic talent and that his unresolved childhood frustrations, unable to find an escape, resulted in the creation of a poltergeist or a disembodied incomplete personality fragment. In other words, it is a suppressed and objectified fragment of the person's personality which has somehow taken on a life of its own.

Whitney himself remains objective. He doesn't know how to explain the ghost. He has his theories, but most important for him is that people understand that ghosts are real.

# Conclusions

As the above twenty-six cases show, ghosts are very real indeed. Their ability to affect the environment is indisputable. They can affect all kinds of electromagnetic equipment. They can turn lights on and off. They can open and close doors, move heavy furniture, make objects disappear. They have the ability to cause all kinds of noises from knockings to crashing sounds. They can also physically manifest as apparitions, or manifest substances, such as cigar smoke or engine oil, or even insects. And as we have seen, ghosts can physically affect people, including pinching, pushing, pulling, hugging, grabbing, choking or in extreme cases, possession.

The accounts are so incredible that one is tempted to accuse the witnesses of lying, hoaxing or misperceiving. However, an analysis of the witnesses reveals a standard-cross section of society including: teachers, housewives, students, secretaries, a bill collector, a waiter, a store owner, actors, a bookkeeper, a dancer, a musician, an artist, a hairstylist, an office worker...the list goes on. The witnesses are very sincere. Most requested anonymity so they're definitely not seeking publicity. Their accounts are also amazingly consistent. For example, in the case of Trudy and Karen, they reported a bizarre problem with their water faucets; witness George Johnson independently reported the exact same problem. It seems unlikely that such an unusual incident could be made up. Furthermore, many of the cases involve multiple witnesses and some involve physical evidence, such as oil stains or dressers blocking doorways. Obviously, these people are seeing something.

An analysis of the above data shows that nearly anybody can see a ghost. One interesting aspect is that many of the ghost witnesses claim to have had other paranormal experiences such as premonitions, precognitive dreams or out-of-body experiences. In at least three cases the ability to see ghosts seems to be inherited. Also the number of female witnesses outnumbers male witnesses about two to one.

The great majority of the hauntings take place in people's modern homes and apartments. Two cases took place at business offices. At least five of the cases took place outside. One took place over a burial ground.

The pattern of the above data shows that ghosts appear virtually everywhere to just about anyone.

Who are the ghosts? Three of the cases involve the ghosts of Native Americans. At least five involve deceased family members of the witnesses. The rest of the cases involve various unknown or non-related male and female ghosts. Three of the cases involve ghosts of children. Two cases involve animal ghosts. Two cases involve suicide victims. Two involve car accident victims. One case involves a disturbed burial ground. One case involves a lady who was killed by fire. Another involves a man who died of emphysema. One involves a man who died of alcoholism.

In many of the hauntings, a death was confirmed. In the other cases, the witnesses did not know if anybody had previously died in the location.

The accounts in this book provide good evidence that something survives the death of the physical body. These are testimonies that simply cannot be pushed aside.

Of course people are seeing ghosts. The question is not, are ghost real, but how do we deal with them?

It is evident from the accounts in this book that ghosts are sometimes aware of their surroundings. They can and do interact with the witnesses. Ghosts, although not physical, are not entirely non-physical either. They do have the ability to affect the environment. As we have seen, they can physically manifest in a huge variety of ways.

If ghosts are able to pick up phones, open and close doors, throw objects across the room and push people, then they obviously are at least partly physical. This movement is evidently done with the astral or spirit body which is made up of a finer material than our physical bodies.

Based on the stories in this book, I believe it is safe to conclude that ghosts are real, and that most ghosts are the spirits of people (or animals) who have died.

What should you do if you have a ghost?

First of all, have no fear. Again, ghosts are only people, and most ghosts are perfectly aware that they have died. If you feel certain that your house is haunted by a lost soul, then probably the best method is to talk to the ghost as if it were a living person. Tell the ghost that he has died and must move into the next dimension where others are waiting for him. Do this especially during or right after there has been a manifestation. Ghosts can hear you and some of the hauntings in this book were resolved in this manner. This will be more effective if you know the ghost's identity.

Prayer is also a method that can be used. In severe cases, hauntings have been resolved by calling in a psychic or a medium who can contact the ghost more easily than the average person, and send it on its way.

If you have a very active poltergeist, this could be the result of emotional stress or perhaps the unwise use of a Ouija board or other occult practice. If this should be the case, bring the issues causing the stress out into the open and discontinue using the Ouija board. As we have seen, poltergeist hauntings can feed off of fear and attention.

Most poltergeist hauntings are short-lived and will go away by themselves. Some, however, seem to become increasingly active and malicious to the point of trying to possess the witness. Some people have found solace through traditional exorcisms, though I think it is important to note that very few of the witnesses in this book found exorcism necessary or effective. Even in the cases where witnesses were nearly possessed, most overcame the problem by ignoring the ghost as much as possible, and conversely ordering it to leave them alone. In every case, the haunting eventually stopped.

Poltergeist attacks usually center around a person who has considerable mediumistic ability. Once the person realizes this, he/she can take steps to learn about their ability, what its limits and potentials are, and how to control it through meditation, and if necessary, block it.

After reading all the above accounts, the reader should have a pretty good idea of what a ghost is, how haunted houses become haunted, and how ghosts affect the environment. So there you have it. Ghosts are real and apparently not uncommon. So next time you hear a strange knocking noise, see a shadow out of the corner of your eye, or feel a strange presence beside you, be ready – you might be encountering an actual ghost!

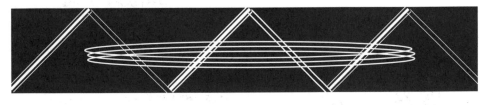

## Endnote

The author is interested in interviewing any other witnesses of paranormal activity. Please contact him at his email address: **prestone@pacbell.net** or write c/o of the publisher.